A flying life

'Life is stranger than fiction'

by

Lloyd Edwards

ISBN: 978-1-300-81753-6

Copyright 2013 © Lloyd Edwards

No part of this publication may be reproduced, stored in a retrieval system, or transmitted, in any form, or by any means, electronic, mechanical, photocopying, recording, or otherwise, without the prior consent of the publisher.

PublishNation | London

www.publishnation.co.uk

We lived at the time near an old disused aerodrome called Manby in Lincolnshire.

I don't know how it all started but safe to say I was the typical nine year old boy who in times past had no access to computers and other 'virtual world' distractions. Most days were spent climbing trees, making camps and in general physical imaginary play. We were not wealthy and I had few toys. One day on a visit to the local DIY shop my Dad purchased us a 'Ping Aeroplane.' This was quite a surprise as the shop stored tools and other DIY house maintenance products. This day on the counter was a cardboard box of polystyrene jet style rubber band catapulted portals of fun! Being one of three boys it was always harder for my Dad to buy toys on limited funds as the cost always escalated three times. We knew not to put Dad in the awkward position of asking for things, so we hoped instead. Well, this day the power of positive thinking paid off and Dad brought us one each.

My twin and older brother did not quite see the magic of flight in the way I did. Yes, they played and enjoyed the 'ping aeroplanes' as any child would but within an hour or so another distraction changed their play. I reached for the sky by standing on the coal bunker and hoped for long flight times. Firing my jet all afternoon till my fingers hurt with elastic recoil! The thrill of it scaling the lofty heights and the scary thought of not quite knowing if I would see it again was all too compelling. Looking back it was not all that dramatic as it stayed within the garden… just! But it was a key moment in the birth of a 'flight life.'

I was born an identical twin which, early on, was great fun. We enjoyed being the centre of attention and soon learned the fun of tricking people as to who was who. We looked so alike my own mother muddled us up most of the time. I would respond to the name Mark and Mark would respond to the name Lloyd. Very early on I was taken into hospital for a hernia operation but it was Mark who needed it! Mum apologised to the Doctor and felt silly having brought the wrong child in. Our first play group/school wanted us separated for development reasons. We enjoyed swopping jumpers and confusing the staff to great effect, it was so exciting. My twin was different to me in many ways. I liked blue but Mark liked yellow. I liked aeroplanes Mark liked boats. Mark was out going and 'the life and soul' and I was the quiet thinker. My twin and I both had dark brown hair from my Nan's side. Also we both had blue eyes. But my older brother, Grant, had brown eyes. I remember secretly peering at these and wondering about them as only a boy of nine could. To describe him to look at would be to say he had brown hair, was thin but strong and being three years older he was always taller.

Grant later went on to build a rubber powered, tissue covered, open geodetic balsa aeroplane of great complexity.

My Dad helped with the build of this rubber powered kit. I remember it was all short lived though as it was damaged on its first flight. I urged for more test flights but my brother had felt the pain of a long build process and was not prepared to risk a further loss. After all, at least he could say 'I built this' and show someone an almost whole aeroplane. We were different in lots of ways like this. Much later in life he was to build a rather large Radio Control Mustang. This was never finished further than one wing and a fuselage. Later my twin and I sat on it by mistake. We did feel terrible at the time considering the work that had gone into it so far. It was left downstairs under a cover because the project had stalled. The project was not 'pushed hard' all the way to its finish. See, building flying models requires a mental push to build to the finish and not stop. One then needs a certain type of courage to risk all the work for flight. Grant had these qualities, but other distractions broke the cycle somehow.

With the pursuit of flight the subsequent smashes can really get you down. Thus it remains; the passion has to be present all the way. After the first mishap the passion takes over and drives one on in a seemingly endless struggle until, one fine day, all is flown and not lost.

At this time, when I was 14 years old, we found ourselves living in a three bedroom house with our Auntie Lucy. We were a family of five living upstairs and Auntie Lucy, the house owner, living downstairs. This arrangement suited us boys because someone was always home when we arrived in from school. Our Auntie Lucy liked to bake and there was always a tasty snack waiting for us. She had white hair, was plump, as all good cooks seem to be, and had soft blue eyes full of smile.

This situation was difficult for my Father who seemed, at the time, to lose his role as head of the family. He had rented homes before this arrangement but money was very tight. This new arrangement was a way to help an ageing aunt keep her house and for us to have cheaper rent. My mother liked the situation because she was able to work more hours and increase the family income. Needless to say Auntie Lucy was a gem of a person and put up with a noisy family in what had been a peaceful home. She proved in many ways to be a wonderful person and is always a fond memory.

I often took to riding my bicycle many miles to find space and free myself from the cramped conditions at home. This was also a time when our relationship as twins was changing. We chose different friends and were just starting *not* to rely on each other for everything. About five miles ride away we had Epsom Downs's race course for equestrian use but, it also had a wide open space in the middle that was used as a local park. A collection of aero modellers used the Downs to fly their Radio Control models. Free flight modellers used the site as well, in the dip, in the centre. In the 1980's Radio Control models were expensive and clever contraptions. Most were built from kits but also 'homebrew designs' were aplenty. I would cycle to the Downs and watch. I would not say too much as I was not the most confident teenager but I would listen, watch and learn. I was often the last person to leave the Downs. I remember picking up the odd broken propeller stub or balsa piece from a past model crash. These shrapnel bits on the floor did not put me off my endeavour. Indeed they were a way of getting closer to these creations. I hatched a plan to build one of these aeroplanes one day and every nugget of information would help me on my way.

These thoughts, the odd sunset and vast dollops of fresh air made the trips very nourishing for an eager young lad. It was very expensive back in those days. So I asked these modellers at the time what was the most cost effective way to get aloft with one of these models. It turned out that gliding from a slope, or 'Slope Soaring', was the cheapest way. The nearest suitable slope was a 14 mile bike ride to Collie Hill near Reigate. We lived in Ashtead, Surrey, so it was quite a trek. Several times I visited the slope but because the wind was blowing in the wrong direction I saw no one. My legs would power me up hill and over dale and even on a small section of dangerous dual carriageway to get to this slope. The excitement of first seeing a collection of chaps freeing these large model gliders from their cars, in the car park and setting off to the hill was inspiring.

Having ridden so far, for the chance to see the action, it was very rewarding. I was amazed to see these models fly, quietly gliding away and rising up, using no fuel, with only the lift from the slope and the odd thermal helping out. Cycling home I was full of zest and peddle power for now I had a new quest that seemed cheaper and therefore within measurable grasp. This would fulfil the goal of flying. A real radio controlled aeroplane! It was not long before a second hand radio and a model glider kit were purchased.

Now I must mention the first Radio Control glider.

Not for the reader's sake only but for my own as well. It is a warm glow that fills me to think of the excitement and hope it gave at the time. It was made by a company called Micro Mold. They were a small, almost cottage engineering, 'bits and widget' supply company. Kitted in a big white cardboard box and showing a drawing of the finished product it was a thrill to stare at this big box with all my hopes and dreams. This box was *all mine* purchased at great cost I might add and represented the whole of my world.

I sold a model railway I had built with my father's help. That represented a year's work. This was dear to me but it was the only thing I owned of value. This new passion was exciting because the stakes were getting high. The model could disappear or crash and it would all be over leaving me without a possession and only comments of 'Well that was a bad choice of spending.' Building the kit was straight forward but required a train journey to purchase the covering film. This, too, was an excursion of note. At that age, it was a new experience to travel by train on my own.

The destination, Mick Charles Model shop in New Malden, was a real treat and one I savoured. Inside people spoke the language I had come to understand and the models hanging up had been used in the Battle of Britain film! Mick Charles himself could be seen but I was served by his son, a keen business man. As I stood there it struck me that this was my adventure, I was buying and I was actually now going to fly. I did all these things on my own as I did the building of the glider. The family were mildly interested but busy with other things just like any other family of five would be. For me it was good to do something on my own. It was also a chance for an adventure to share and a new story to tell.

On an earlier cycle ride to the hill slope I had noted the poplar trees behind our house bending with the wind. I soon recognised that these trees would indicate whether or not it was worth the long cycle trek to the slope. The wind had to be blowing on a southerly heading to guarantee lift at the 'Collie Hill' slope soaring site, so these trees saved me many a wasted journey. This early lesson of recognising the wind's direction is still a habit today.

One particular aero modeller let me have a short time controlling his model high up. I shall never forget the honour and thrill. He was the only one to do this since the models were hard to make and costly. No one really lets you have a go, particularly as a child. I had spent many hours looking and feeling on the outside of things with these guys. This little episode made me feel included and gave me real incentive and a little confidence too. Because of this experience this act of sharing has followed me in my life and has motivated me to share the gift of flight. Full size or model flying, it is great fun sharing the excitement and I make a note to do such at all times when anyone shows the slightest interest.

So, getting back to the log, I completed the build and then was challenged as to how I was going to get my creation to the site without breaking it. With enough will anything is possible and not a lot can stand in the way of passion. So off I set on my bicycle with my 'Micro Mold Cub Glider' and second hand radio in a purpose made back pack. When I arrived there was no one there and it took some time for me to muster up courage to throw it out into the air. The hill was some seven hundred feet high. Well, I needn't have worried since the wind was square on to the slope, 'dead ahead' as they say. This created the needed lift for glider flight.

Up she rose and flew straight out. The steady way it climbed with such ease was sheer class in my book. Yet this was base one, aero modelling, at budget level. Very soon a safe height was reached for me to try turning. Gulp! Height is a great safety net with a model, but soon one has to come down. I had no flight experience only my reading of books and magazines. So turn I had to and I did this by nudging the controls. I must add this works to a point, but is not really the best way. I had no real circuit plan and needless to say my landing back at the slope was an arrival! As I ran over to see the damage I remember being relieved to have it arriving back on the hill and not flying miles away.

The thought of how far it had flown was amazing and I skipped in a childish way, full of glee, back to the bits. No one was around to congratulate me but also, no one was around to make fun. It was not all that bad as only the fuselage had been split. That was all for that day because no one was there to show me how to fly. It was just as well another flight did not take place as it would have ended in greater disaster, I'm sure. It crashed right by a small Hawthorn bush that stood alone and is still there to this day and so X marks the spot for me at least.

I was no scholar and to read anything other than what interested me was no real pleasure. I was not a book worm. Our schooling was sporadic and a little topsy turvy. We went to first school, like most children but soon were taken out of it to be 'home schooled.' This was in 1970 and my parents being free thinkers thought it best for our morals and best for our education. Home economics was my Mum getting us to tidy round making the beds and helping with the dinner. Dad would take us through science lessons and it did not take long to get through the curriculum. We liked it because we had more time to make camps and play outside. After several house moves this all came to a close. The study was also getting hard for

Mum and Dad to fit it all in. Work pressed them into longer hours and so our home school came to an end.

So it was not long and we went back to school. By the time we entered Comprehensive school we had a shock. The school we went to as teenagers was a big school with 1400 children. It had some problems and it was a far cry from 'home school' or 'first schools.' My twin and I turned up with knitted jumpers on, not knowing what a 'pop chart' was or anything else our peers were interested in. The kids were into early designer clothes and Michael Jackson. By this time we had no television either and had missed out on most of the opening discussions that the kids used. Needless to say we were bullied because we were different and stood out. The main three bullies were from Borstal remand school. The Headmaster was an old softy who felt his school was their only chance to get a break in life and so tolerated more than he should from these individuals. They later beat up a lad who did not recover from his injuries. Luckily for our Headmaster it happened off school premises and the school managed to wriggle out of any attachment to the tragic incident.

My parents were out working hard most of the time, but did take out time to come in and to see the old Headmaster about the bullying. He was stuck with his views and nothing changed. My Mum used to wrap my shins in 'witch hazel' soaked bandages to bring out the bruises in the evening and I would go in for more of the same the next day.

I befriended similar types of misfits like a Vietnamese boat refugee child from China, who was bullied as well. He went on to learn serious martial arts and strangely the bullying stopped after this. So these early experiences taught me self reliance and that the larger group could often miss out on interesting individuals. My friend was a most interesting guy who could barely speak English but was a true companion. This is relevant to flying models because it was something unique to me at the time. I was beginning to learn early in life, not to take things or people at face value.

I remember also at this time my only true purchase book wise was; 'Dave Hughes Slope Soaring.' This was a magical book that I carried around with me and it helped transcend a rough time at School. It was information to dwell on when all the others were off playing and I was left alone. I would even read it, in a boring part of a lesson. The teacher had a job disciplining and organising the class which took time, so I would sneak a read on how best to launch a glider or such.

The Headmaster later retired and a different set of values were introduced. I'm glad to say; I hear it is not a bad school at all these days. Sometimes change is a very good thing.

The next time I went up to the hill to fly my new Cub glider, there were some modellers who tried to fly my model. This was with little success creating more damage. You see the second hand radio was 'split stick' for car and boat use, so one had two levers to control up down, left and right. The convention is one stick to do both. With 'my tail between my legs' at the end of the day, I went home with the advice to buy a proper radio transmitter. My teenage funds were well depleted so I could not buy the better radio transmitter, but I did have about seven flights of the cub. Even with a poor controller the thrill was immense and still warms me to think of it today.

You cannot beat looking up into the majestic heavens of sanctity and space, beholding your small creation within it. Sky is so pretty and vast. It is not often we spend an hour or so looking into it, seeing the huge corridors between billowing white cloud mass. Lift in sky, presents itself in many different ways and the model shows up all its complexity. The skill needed has to be honed to complete a good soaring flight. The action is full on and demanding most of the time. There is a lovely combination of achievement interest and beauty to be had with this style of model flying. One can always relax after the flight and watch the others fly with stunning scenery all around.

A few years later, many hours of pre secular work for the teenager now fifteen and another trip to the model shop. I had saved money from gardening work with Grant which was all hard graft. This time I was going all the way with my purchases at Mick Charles Models. To put it into perspective, at the time a second hand car could be purchased for the same cost of my Radio control power plane complete. Not a good car; but a car! Complete with an MOT and road tax. (Electronics have come down in price relative to earnings today).

My newly built model which took six months to complete I hasten to add, was now ready for the Downs.

Grant new the effort involved and came with me to cheer me on for my first power flight. With full throttle set and full hope in heart, up it went in a full power takeoff. Then the 'on and off switch' failed, which was fitted through the balsa fuselage. The fuselage had not been cut out well enough allowing the 'on and off switch' for the onboard receiver, to only just be on. With the vibration of full power in the climb the switch turned off. I lost Radio contact and it looped a massive full power loop, right round upside down, then bang! Into the ground it went with terrific force to end in smithereens. Six months work and all my hopes over in thirty seconds flat.

It took me a while to recover as it was not the money but the love and time taken to build it. My twin brother was very damning of the endeavour to fly toy planes, but all this did not put me off. I had some success with the glider and had worked out *why* the fault had occurred. I was discovering that flying aircraft was as good as the weakest link. Unlike a car or boat, the fixing cannot always take place before catastrophe strikes. Everything has to be spot on in the build and design and then and only then; one can struggle with the air, with confidence in the aeroplane at least.

After this episode a new airframe was purchased and built and the parts from the crashed aeroplane reused, like the motor and radio. I flew again with a new 'Cessna high wing, full house trainer.' This time I was all by myself, so vital checks could be carried out without rushing. I also had a better awareness of getting everything spot on with build and indeed flight operation. I had several good flights and being young picked things up very fast. Landing was very forgiving in the long corn only my depth perception was off with this, my ninth flight.

I flew into a tree and had to climb up it, to get to the model. It was a huge tree and my model had come to rest the very top. The trouble was that it came to rest up in the finer foliage that I could not climb.

So I had to precariously stand on an upper limb and shake it down. Damage was bad to the airframe after this shake down and subsequent fall from the tree. Another loss but lots of lessons learned and greater flight time had.

It took till I started work to get another airframe ready and this 'Parasol vintage style aeroplane' finished off my flying training. It was purchased at Sussex Model Centre in Worthing Sussex, another great train ride. I was not a great flyer but I could drive it round on a quite windless day to some accuracy. At this time I had say twenty flights to my name with models but full size aeroplanes would get in the way of this pursuit.

Later at school were we given the opportunity for work experience, one week before 'half term.'

I remember the teacher saying to us in our final year that. "Each person will be allocated a job outside school. This will be for one week to see what is expected in the work environment." This was a great scheme to help us sixteen year old kids learn about what was ahead, so it was less of a shock. I hated school by this time and looked forward to work, where you could at least *not* be beaten up.

Then my heart sank as I remember the teacher reading out retail shops and offices etc. that the other children would go to. Only half the class had allocation and I quickly asked what would happen to the rest of us. Finding enough employers would be hard, but everyone would get somewhere allocated to them. We were also to complete an essay on our work placement experience. As the class shuffled out for lunch I asked the teacher what all the forms were and how it worked. Our teacher said "We give these to the employer, they sign them and then we send you to work." Seeing that the work load was high for the teacher I stole a form when she was not looking. I intended to go to somewhere I wanted to go rather than being sent to somewhere I didn't want to go. It would help their work load and they may be pleased, I thought, justifying my actions in some way.

I jumped on my bicycle and rode in our lunch hour to Rushett Farm Chessington. I rode like I was being chased by the police and having a form in my hand that was not meant for me, it felt like it too. This ride in one hour and back was 'mission impossible' with the long distance involved. But my bike and I were old adventurers that could and did cover many miles. You see over the back of where we lived I noticed the occasional real aircraft on descent, approaching what was a farmer's field. I made enquires and set off by foot to explore this place days before. It was a 'one man band' aircraft restoration company. Geoff Masterton had struck a deal to use a farmer's field as a runway and repair/restore old aircraft in a converted barn. Now, I loved flight but to see a real aeroplane up close and touch it was something else. And so it was that I cycled to this place having been once before, but having never spoken to anyone about it.

When I arrived there was a new Port a Cabin built as an office and the door was shut. I was scared to go in but holding an official form and school to face later, had to. What was the point of all this crazy effort? Out of breath, I braved it and opened the door. It was very stressful for me as an aircraft owner pilot was talking to the main man Geoff. I was in a hurry but waited politely as I was on his turf. I had learnt to listen and pick things up quickly, so I soon realised who was who in the conversation between customer and proprietor. When I was noticed Geoff asked "What *do you want*?" with some cynicism. He was a thick set strong man whose dark hair was balding through stress no doubt, but he had a kind face that was very open.

He had obviously seen many young 'wannabe' plane spotters in his time and needed to work without these types of people clogging things up. But his knowing smile meant he had tolerance as I'm sure he was the same when he was young. I went bright red but managed to blurt out with great urgency the need for him to sign this school form and I would do anything asked of me. I explained I could clean the aeroplanes and make tea, anything. He must have seen my desperation. Still puzzled but wanting to get back to his client, he signed my form. I was so nervous I could not take it in nor stay. I said "thank you" and cycled away before he changed his mind. Half way up the track what had just happened slowly sank in.

YES! I was going to spend a week around real aircraft and real pilots! I would hear the tales of real pilots and ask lots of questions. I would have something to talk about at home too. In a busy house with many goings on and issues it is nice to have something to talk about that belongs to you alone at this age. As I cycled back a reality of how the teachers would take this started to sink in. Perhaps they would not let me go? Perhaps they would notice I was late too. Blimey! I could be in serious trouble. Looking at my watch I *was* in some form of trouble. After being told off for being late to the next lesson I lost courage to say what I had done and slipped the form in the pile that was on the table. I hoped the teachers did not notice this odd addition. Guess what they didn't!

Remarkably my first work experience aged 16 still at school was at Light Aircraft Services Chessington. Geoff was kind to spotters, young dreamers and all air brained people. I was sure, at the time, that this was the career for me and yet he was pivotal into me *not* taking up light aircraft engineering. He advised me early in the week that computers were all the rage and that this restoration was a vocation that some people did for free. Geoff struggled as an underdog restoring aircraft almost for the love of it. A year or so later with a family and all the business he did have a heart attack and died on the job. Such is the harshness of life.
On a positive side we did have a great time in this place and because of Geoff. I say *we*, as two old retired chaps were also always there and came to help out. A qualified engineer worked for real money with Geoff being the boss. The qualified engineer later went on to work for B.A. and we met up through involvement in a little red aeroplane. More on this thread later.
On my first week time was spent, making tea and I even helped with some crack testing on a real undercarriage. I set some wood bits on Auster's stringers to the fuselage to hold the fabric out. All this was under strict supervision of course. I did make two mistakes in the work place mind. One day I managed to set the cups one side of the washing up bowl and drag the kettle lead into the water consequently knocking out the power to the hanger and office. On another day I was instructed to paint over the black dots a spider's

poop made on a newly covered Tiger Moth. This was originally painted with a spray gun to a first class finish in WW2 colours olive drab and dark earth camouflage. I diligently painted over the dots being given the wrong colours!

There was physical relief from the stress of embarrassment and great excitement to be had as well. When an aircraft flew in for a check or service the incoming pilot would telephone Geoff and I would keep an ear open for the sound of them flying overhead. The strip was mega short with heavy power lines one end and a ditch the other. I would run down to the field and remove the cattle wire so they could taxi in quick as a flash. Previous the aircraft would have to circle and watch for the older guys to saunter over and clear the way in. This was so exciting for me and amazing to be really close to a real aeroplane. What noise! What magic!

Back in the main workshop, pinned to the wall, were pictures of a crashed twin engine aeroplane. This white twin Comanche stood at the entrance of the site looking very sorry for its self with no hope of flying. It was an effigy or statue to Insurance wincing out on the deal. Geoff himself also featured in the crash pictures, a local paper giving the shots. Having suffered an engine failure in a Currie Wot biplane his emergency landing was high in the tree tops. There was a dense wood opposite to the South of the strip. A lucky escape at the time, as he landed plumb on top of the trees, neither plunging down nor falling out of them. It was just like my model in the corn field a few years prior only this being full size. It was clever flying to slow it down so and a good dollop of luck I hasten to add.

In my mind this place was a gold mine of information, tales and everything stimulating beyond in the outside world. Looking back it was an interesting place for any age and a type that is fast fading. One of the reasons compelling me to write this down is to try, in some way, to capture what was. We often think what we know now, to be different to the past and so this is a snippet of history in a way all be it a small one.

I was invited to stay the next half term week which was an honour and relief as the time raced by. I was having such a great time!

Although having been given the lecture not to do this as a career I knew, somehow, I was in a window of opportunity.

A pilot called Peter Kinsey showed up to air test the old Tiger Moth that had been recovered. He owned a 'Cosmic Wind Ballerina' aircraft which at the time was in bits. I car polished all these bits for him and being painted in dark metallic green they came up well. I had not met real pilots before and so saw them as way up there. He was slightly strange as he was young, but balding in a way you expect older people to. I suspected at that time that was because he was clever in my ignorance of the adult world. I was right in some way for he was the cleverest pilot I ever knew and to this day the chief display pilot at Duxford. He was not that tall or stocky just a medium size chap. The guys whispered to me that he was a great flyer at the time. I was in awe of him and as a teenager could not set about a long conversation. I smiled at him and listened to conversations he had with the others. Sadly he was in and out a lot, which was a shame, because he had some stories to tell. The old guys soon filled me in on what he had flown and done.

One of the old guys walked with a limp. I asked too many questions sometimes and was taken aside once to be told not to mention the limp. I asked why and was told he spun a Tiger Moth in and killed the passenger. Turns out this old guy had the wreckage in a barn behind and talked of restoration. I was told that he never would rebuild it and was not in a good financial position to have it rebuilt by someone else. 'He should sell the bits and move on,' I was told. The limp was a crash injury and I asked no more of it. He was a small silver haired guy who was always funny in a cynical way but spoke about flying as though he was a current pilot. I did sneak a peek of the wrecked bits of his Tiger Moth in the barn behind. It did look creepy all smashed in and quietly rotting away.

In the week Pete Kinsey flew the camouflaged Tiger Moth and said it handled badly though neither him nor Geoff knew why since it had been set correctly by the book. Our old silver haired chap, with the limp, held the key with some very sound advice and knowledge on rigging up the Tiger Moth. He did this with fine adjustment being carried out using tuning forks to the flying wires and changes to the wing incidence. This sort of practice is dying out with his generation and was very interesting to watch.

Another odd thing to happen was a connection made at the farm with another chap who telephoned me three years later. He asked me if I wanted the bits to a restored Moth Major for nine thousand pounds, a bargain at the time. As I was about 19 at the time with little capital I refused the offer. Looking back what an offer it was. Life is full of 'what if' scenarios and past connections.

The final story of note from Rushetts Farm was on my last day Peter Kinsey showed up asking for a battery. He was to drive to White Waltham aerodrome and fit it to an aircraft. Everyone smiled knowingly at me as we drove off. This was the first time I was invited to go out by adults in my own right. Being treated like an adult was great but still I held a little self consciousness as only teenagers do.

Then Geoff sprang it on me. I was to fly in a De Havilland Chipmunk back to Rushetts Farm after the battery was fitted, with Pete Kinsey.

I was nervous, excited and almost having an 'out of body experience.' Before I knew it I was being strapped in. My straps were tightened and I held my first camera that followed me those days wherever I went. Photos were expensive in those days so people generally only shot one or two. So I only have two photos of this memorable day. I was told about holding on tight to my camera and briefed on basic flight controls. Having flown models all was simple in this regard, but I wondered why my harness was so tight, I was soon to find out. I was a day dreamer and was soon thinking of the chaps in WW2 with a cockpit so similar in style and look. It was a harsh and slightly creepy interior being painted black. This was made worse with me imagining warfare and such like. See, the old Chippy was in 1950's RAF trainer colours and the pilots sit in tandem like many WW2 cockpit layouts. In light aviation the Chipmunk is often mentioned as a poor man's Spitfire.

All creepiness soon disappeared as off we took into the evening sun which was so pretty. It was not as I expected. I had never flown in an aeroplane before, only sat in one. Flying was noisy and surreal. The outside picture didn't convey the reality of height. It's not like climbing a ladder or such. You could see the ground, but with everything looking so small and dainty it seemed another world. A pretty dreamlike world, all be it a noisy one.

It was not long before I was given the controls. I was so nervous but did reasonably well in turning and flying level. That was enough for me and nerves made me want to widdle again. I had not wanted to say about going for the loo prior as time was against the flight with the sun setting. So I was happy sitting high and in a real plane and could now talk about it to friends and family. Wonderful great smashing and terrific! That was till we came across Wisley Aerodrome near Guildford a disused WW2 bomber runway good for lining up aerobatics.

Pete wanted to brush up on a display routine and asked me if it was ok to do some aerobatics. I said yes wanting to please and not knowing the true effects. We ended up doing a full aerobatic ground display at zero feet. Plus four positive G and minus two negative G! All this with the pullout from the manoeuvres, say 20 feet up, no more. For anyone that has not done this it is odd and not pleasant. For G (or effect of gravity multiplied) in that, if you weigh 12 stone, at four G you now weigh 48 stone! It feels like you are going to fall through the bottom of the seat. It feels like the whole aircraft is going to fold its wings. That your cheeks are folding over like a cartoon character of a Bulldog. The blood rushes into your boots and with time you start tunnel vision to black out. I nearly did but being fit carried on feeling the bad effects. Unlike fairground rides the G input to the body is prolonged. With negative G you get a slight red vision as blood is forced into your head and eyes. Fortunately for me the Chippy could only take a little negative G.

I remember following what we were doing but nearly passing out. The ground rushed up often and in the end I, mentally, gave up. I watched the ground roll round and round the canopy every which way with the fate of my life in his hands. I did not feel sick only I wanted to go to the toilet so my kidneys hurt. When we landed it was relief which was a shame. I started out enjoying the flight but ended up pleased just to be alive. The guys back at the Farm were waiting anxiously to see my face and response to my first ever flight. They wanted me to have had the best time which was kind. I remember feeling honoured but could not respond only dash to the loo. They all thought it was because I felt sick, but it was just to relieve myself. I thought then that pilots like Pete were a little odd to like G forces and aerobatics. Perhaps *I was not like them* at all. Also at that point I liked aeroplanes, but was nervous about flying in them. I raced home on my bicycle at night as time had moved fast. I had quite a day to recount.

Life is stranger than fiction and I have only started to realise this, looking back.

The more I went on the flying journey the stranger it became. My next full size experience came when I had left school and was working with B.T. this was by accident. Before I begin it is worth noting the model aircraft had been dormant though, it did help me get my first job. Having been warned off the light aircraft engineering I decided to go for a job and become a postman.

I went for the interview with my father going for the same position too. We sat in the same room for the short test which was odd but nice to spend time together. I did get the job perhaps by being younger. I went to the sub post office to talk to the guys about what it was *really* like. I was told by the main guy not to go for it and to aim higher. I walked home puzzling on the information and soon thought, 'how about motor engineering.' It must be similar to aeroplane engineering and a workshop environment too.

I thought I would aim high and work down the list with this job hunting again, so Rolls Royce it was. We had a small franchise in Ashtead and so I thought I'd grab my Radio Control planes and go and see them. Later they said it was so funny to see a young lad come up the ramp into the workshop with his model planes uninvited. For my part it was a little nerve wracking but what was the harm in asking.

The partners were impressed oddly by this and made an apprenticeship just for me. It was the best job ever and I only left to gain a career. This business was a family partnership and a closed shop for future progression beyond mechanic. Who knows if it was the right decision? They went on to weather the large car market storm and still trade today. I would have been happier in my day to day work but not ended up owning my own home. They say those who do not know what they want to do end up living the most interesting lives, a small conciliation. Who knows? We make decisions at the time with the information given and live guided by these tenuous pivotal moments.

I left a year later, not knowing what a big company was like to work for and soon found out. I moved up the ladder quickly, four promotions in five years to technical Officer. It was a challenge but not vastly interesting or exciting. I mean who can get excited about cable and connectors? But it was real life and a steep challenge. I thrived on 'mission impossible' by now and did well for a youngster. I had the time and energy but something was always missing.

One day I went to meet friends on a Ferry crossing day trip to France. Not my thing really, only there were youngsters my age going and it was good to have a rare opportunity to mix in a group like this. I set off early but became caught in traffic. I arrived; to literally see the ship depart yards away. I waved at people on deck hoping it was my friends so we could at least laugh at that moment later on. It was a long way this Dover and so I had a day to myself now unplanned which was rare for me. It was summer and it was not long before I was looking up at the sky. I noticed two gliders in the distance and looking at the map guessed it was Challock Gliding Club. So I drove towards the circling gliders and soon found the field.

My heart always skipped as I drove up to airfields it is a bit like getting near to the sea when you know you are there because of the lack of horizon on approach to it. The gliders were all laid out and the winch was active as was some aerial towing. I went in the club house for some tea and a chat. It was a good thermal day with white puffy clouds like small bombs going off and brilliant blue all around. It was around two o'clock in the afternoon.

I love club rooms with their makeshift approach. Interesting maps on the wall, club adverts, and the latest curling photo with; 'Purchase this plane' written below. You see relics of the past, lying around, bits of instrument or whatever perhaps a radio tuned to the airfield frequency. You can often find the comforts of good British tea and the odd home bake. This one had the lot and I felt pleased now I had missed the ferry and come this way. I needed to see if I did like flying as a pilot or passenger come to think of it. At this point I was not sure after my extreme aerobatic experience. So I asked for a flight.

I had cash on me and asked for a lesson and aero tow. As I had 'proper cash' and the club funds were low I was fast tracked and airborne in a Slingsby K13 before the hour had passed.

We set out over the South Downs near Canterbury being aero towed by a power plane. I did ask what the parachute was for and was told "Gliders are weaker by design, anyway you need at least 1500 ft to use it and below this you're stuffed!" Charmin! I thought this is helping me lose my nerves? "They're pointless unless you collide high up anyway most people undo their shoot in the panic with their seatbelt. You do need a chute 'off the winch' and then you are too low, so, just think of it as a comfy cushion!" I was now a little nervous pre-flight, but once airborne I began to relax a little and enjoy it. It must be the stunning sights that meet your eyes but somehow the fear soon melts away. I loved tracking sidewise across the Downs crabbing into wind looking down. It felt a bit like my model flying only with very different views. The gliders did seem to congregate in the same areas so I could see how collision was a small risk. I suppose I was not completely relaxed but somewhere in between. Still, in control was good and I enjoyed every minute all feelings balanced.

This was great news as now I could think about getting into full size flying as a hobby. I flew a few flights with the club later on but it was a long way to travel from home. Also it takes several people to get a glider up, so there was lots of hanging around and once I went all the way to Kent with no flight to be had. I'm now of the opinion that one needs to live near a gliding site and preferably be retired or easy with time, to indulge in gliding. It is one of the best types of flying though if you do have the circumstances.

I did do a silly thing one day stretching out the glide, to take the heat from a burning hay barn.

I could see the smoke way off and so tip toed out from the slope lift on shallow descent in hope of hot air lift. As I lost height the smoke was showing me the way and beckoning me on. It was not good to land away from the airfield as it was hard to de-rig the glider and get it safely back. Also it could be dangerous landing in a field with concealed obstacles like cattle wires or ditches. By the time I arrived over the lift, the old K13 had lost valuable height and yes the lift saved me, but cinders and smoke were a new issue. I was unprepared for the extreme rough force of this type of lift. I suddenly thought; 'fabric and dope coverings are highly flammable' the dope smell is a form of gas. Having now been given the healthy blast of lift with the cinders swirling around the glider I was sent chasing back to the airfield praying I was not on fire.

The only other story to say about the gliding at Challock was a new neighbour decided to build a house on the approach to the runway that had been there years. Then he complained about the glider noise! Well all gliders make a pleasant swish noise, not loud at all, especially with the speed back on finals to land. This noise was rarely audible above the spot of his new house, which was built right on the approach path to land. The runway had been there years and so the question rose, if he hated the aircraft why build right under them? As I left one day I could see he was busy erecting a mast to the chimney pot of his house for a weather vane.

I received a great phone call telling me of a 'hot shot' glider pilot who managed to swoop low with his glass ship and clout the weather vane in protest. There was damage to the wing but the pilot could afford the repair to it. I laughed at the time but later thought it was luck he did not crash it could have gone horribly wrong. It is the way with aviation, most times it is all adventure and fun but sometimes it does go wrong with disastrous consequences. Much later I did read about a mid air collision at Challock which was very sad as it resulted in the loss of young life. I was yet to gain a healthy fear of flying but did so, on a Cessna 152, in the United States.

By the end of my B.T. days I was doing well secularly but not so well stress wise.

Sunday left me with a headache and I knew B.T. was not the right life career. It may have been if I had stuck as an engineer but I had boxed myself into a difficult position, planning large business customer installations. I worked around south London with major projects. B.T. was half in the past with a workforce who felt the company was a second home or owed them in some way. B.T. was now competing against A.T.& T and Mercury, it was riding on its past Laurels somewhat. Without being boring, it was not looking good and time for me at least, to bail out. There were redundancy murmurings and aviation was calling me.

Months before I decided to gain a Private Pilots Licence at Redhill Aerodrome. I paid my £100 per hour brought the books and on weekends sat in Cessna 152's learning to fly. I was still *slightly* wondering if piloting was for me, in a detached way. After ten hours training I realised I was learning 10 to 15 minutes of what was learnt the week before! It was not too efficient considering the costs. I discovered that flying as a pilot *was* for me after about eight hours and thought I best save the whole amount to get the licence in one hit. Having taken all the exams prior it was now all about the flying. 'Best stop and save me thinks.'

Well, I looked into set courses in Alderney near Jersey. These were advertised in pilot magazines and such. It was pointed out that if the weather was bad it was a waste of money as continuity was the issue. I saw adverts for flying in Texas USA and thought this the best route, due to better weather alone. I would now have to learn two theory exams, particularly air law being different. Still it was done and I remember selling everything. I mean everything to get the funds. Car, record player, leather jacket, R/C planes the lot.

I had been on a jet plane once before, a quick hop on a holiday charter 737 paid for by Grant. This quick holiday had been to Malta, just the two of us. But now, this was the first time on my *own* travelling abroad to the U.S.A. on a 747 Jumbo Jet. At the check in desk, I was upgraded to Club class. Things like this happened in early 1991. My parents were very supportive of any hair brained scheme we boys came up with and they were both there, to see me off. My Dad was reported to cry slightly at Gatwick airport as they said goodbye. I was too caught up in the adventure to notice any emotions of affection in anyway. I did not miss home or family because it was all well; quite a ride.

Arit Air Academy was the name of the establishment I paid my hard earned money into.

A few thousand pounds and it was hard come by. A 'black guy' in an older American car met and greeted me at Dallas international. He took me to Redbird Municipal Airport just outside Dallas. He was easy to talk to and it turned out he was the owner of the academy. We new students had a strange boastful tour round and something then did not quite fit, although at the time I could not place it. As the sun set we were shown to these awful grotty, somewhat dangerous, apartments with cockroaches and gang drug dealings going on all around. There was no air-conditioning that worked and no linen on the beds. These were bad apartments in a bad end of town.

I was billeted with an ex army helicopter pilot going for his commercial licence. He had been there for weeks. First thing in the morning we poured over maps at the airport and I got my head around the different way it was done over the pond. I flew one hour in the morning and one hour in the evening. The air was calmer at this time as the noon temperature reached 110 degrees and the turbulence was horrendous. I did try to fly once and once only, in the mid day heat. The turbulence was so bad I could not see the instruments and I thought my teeth would fall out! The seat belt was essential and had to be on tight over ones lap. Never again!

I was doing *reasonably* well with the training first off. Only, I was with a very placid Swedish instructor who was too calm and kind. I started to pick up in conversation that he had not been paid recently. We flew into a golf Course as only one can in America. It was really bizarre the way the golf trolleys seem to taxi round with personal aeroplanes. The approach pad says for pilots to 'Lookout for Golf balls!' If you did see a golf ball hurtling your way, how were you supposed to make your aeroplane duck? I remember thinking.

At breakfast I could only watch my instructor eat his food as my money was going on hidden extras like fuel. The Arit Air Academy had not paid its fuel bills, neither the fees for the flight exam tests with the FAA. I had only a fixed amount to live off. A Lady overheard our conversation about the club and its customer problems. She quickly went home and as we left, presented me with a pillow and some sheets for the bed. I said I could not return them as this was a cross country flight and declined the offer. She said "Take them dear, I don't want you to go back home with the wrong view of the United States." That blew me away, such open kindness to me a complete stranger.

When I arrived back at base it was my last flight with the Swedish guy. I went down the road and with my last 10 dollars brought food for the two weeks remaining of the three week course. I brought white sesame seeded baps, made for burgers, in a huge bin bag. I purchased plastic cheese and a strange relish to ease it down. I swore that relish glowed in the dark! I also brought cornflakes, tea bags and a water bottle as the site had a water fountain. My weight went from thirteen stone down to nine and a half on this new diet.

I was mugged at knife point in Dallas downtown changing buses for the pilot medical. I later learned; looking at a map, and lost late in the evening, is an invite to be mugged. I was not 'street wise' at this time in life. It is all about what street you are *in* not the larger area in the U.S.A. I had two savings that day; one was my British accent which brought me time, the other was a taxi driver. He saved me by driving over with the passenger door flung open, for me to dive into the back seat. Which I did, this must have looked like some '1970's TV cop soap opera.' The taxi driver drove me all the way to the Redbird airport for no charge, so again a second person showing extreme kindness.

This mugging at knife point was one of three times in my life I was truly scared as these guys were high on drugs and it could have gone either way. My life was totally in *their* control. Another time was soon to follow.

Now this next turn of events gave me a healthy scare and made me respect flying at all times afterwards.

As with all bad decisions and accidents, there are many incidents leading up to the event. The Civil Aviation Authority publishes figures from the accident investigation bureau, stating that there are seven bad events leading up to most accidents. These are telling 'tell tale' signs in prevention to the big bang and I will mention this later.

Well the day came for my solo cross country and as funds for fuel were only just on track, I elected to fly high for efficiency. I looked up the performance log with the temperature of the day. I forget the exact height I was going to fly at but it was high for maximum fuel burn. Next I set a course on the map, to fly my cross country triangle to Oklahoma. I would fly northwards on to a small derelict airstrip, then onto a large military aerodrome eastwards. Finally back home south, to Redbird. As a student, I passed right over Dallas Fort Worth International Airport, with its seven large runways!

The Americans are more trusting with light aviation and tend to mix up commercial traffic with private traffic. Space is the reason and I enjoyed the trust I was given. It could be less safe for commercial traffic mind, but let's not get into that.

So after Fort Worth, I sat the first two hour leg, in complete boredom. I had filed a flight plan and onwards towards Oklahoma there was nothing to do. There was no one to talk to on the radio just the drum of the engine. At least it was cooler up here. So my plan to get down for the landing was to spin the plane down. It is the quickest way down *but* 'a little bit of knowledge is a dangerous thing.' I had spun gliders before and the procedure was, to raise the nose into the stall. A pre-stall buffet is felt and with full up held in; one slides the rudder hard over. The glider will spin down quite gently and rather flat in a stall, until recovered. Simple.

With the Cessna in full cruise, I pulled the throttle back and was impatient to remain level and let it stall. I raised the nose with a progressive yank on the yolk. The flying speed was still too high and in my impatient pull, I saw the ground again from behind my head! On top of this odd manoeuvre the stall Warner horn went off, giving me the false feeling I had stalled. Or it could have been the angle of attack too high, but I had not stalled. These Warner horns are set to go off, about 10% above the stall speed. I understood later, to go by *feel* is always better. I had not had one of these devices in the glider. I am not blaming the stall Warner, as my entry into the spin was very wrong and it was all a severe case of 'a little knowledge is a dangerous thing.'

Somewhere upside down I kicked in full rudder and held it in with the full up. What I *had* done was a half loop into a spiral dive. Now a spiral dive is very different to a spin, with speed rising rapidly and the aircraft flying, but screaming downhill. I was alarmed at the speed increase with the throttle shut. The gauge had a 149 knots VNE (never exceed speed) then it had 160kts, then a black space to start again at the beginning. This needle kept on going! My concentration was soon on the pullout. The airflow forced the prop to high RPM even though the throttle was shut. I knew I could not pull too much G in pulling out of this horrendous dive. The pullout from the spiral dive took way too long. I had felt G before and knew I could not add much more. In retrospect and with aerobatic knowledge now, I should have rolled the wings level at the top of the half loop. But right now I was at a point of no return.

Just prior to this attempted spin, I climbed a little and it was just as well as the ground came up alarmingly and dangerously close. The screen split and I knew it was close to tearing the wings off. What was puzzling was my leg was still shaking when I finally levelled out. I had held the rudder in slightly the whole time in panic. Yes this was the second and only time I have been *really* scared. As I took my feet off the rudder pedals, the tail shook and she was not tracking straight. I was on short finals to my destination before I knew it. I landed with a feeling of extreme relief. When I got out, I saw the rivets had popped one side of the fuselage and some ripples in the skin on the other. The control horns of the rudder had collapsed in and it was all floppy. I had flown at slow speed to this destination as the rudder would not take more. At least the Cessna held up and still did fly along.

Now I should not have flown it further, but all I could think was I have no money to get to Redbird! So I better fly off before anyone sees this aeroplane *and* perform a touch and go at the next airport, so no one stops me or reports me. I topped up with fuel, signed in the register and took off with the damaged stricken bird. I flew to the next Airport and did a 'smartish' touch and go, to get the cross country in officially. On the way home I burnt more fuel than planned and oddly stayed low, as it felt safer. This was another naive decision but I got away with all the mistakes.

As I was slow, the sun was setting when I came back to base. I remember one could click the runway lights like a dimmer switch with the transmit button on the yolk. This was done with the approach frequency set. America is full of easy flying gimmicks' and plush airfields with no landing fees it is very 'private aircraft friendly.' I felt much calmer now the flight was over and pleased to be back. At the end of this flight I wanted to tell someone the whole sorry tale and relieve some of the last stress. I went to the hanger and signed off the aircraft as un-airworthy. A mechanic was packing up and as I approached him he blew up about not being paid or caring about the aircraft anymore. Slamming his tools around I thought he was best left alone. I did not get my story out to him or anyone else that day. I put a note in the aeroplane to say 'Un-airworthy' which was silly as you could clearly see it was un-airworthy!

The very next day an instructor from the German Luftwaffe; young trim and fresh from his F16 Jet fighter, was looking over the sorry Cessna. He was associated with the academy and was kicking around right now. I sheepishly told him the story. He forcefully commanded me to get in the other club Cessna 152 and to be taught how to spin properly. As we taxied out he told me that the owner of the academy was now on the run from the IRS for tax evasion and that if I worked hard, he would try to get me my PPL. He was a great tutor for me as he was not kind and 'wishy washy,' but firm with his instruction and very clear. This suited my somewhat 'day dream mind' much better. We flew and flew and drilled the lessons hard. By a week and a half I had passed, with 40.2 hours exact, thanks to him.

The other members were left confused and worried about their money. No one else had any flying training for their investments. I left the course with five dollars only in my pocket and some three days ahead of the allotted three weeks. I now had a shiny new F.A.A. Private Pilots Licence. This incidentally was the size of a credit card which seemed a shame to me considering all the effort. I was the only one in that course date with a licence. I counted myself lucky; very lucky, the Luftwaffe had seen me through!

Life back in Blighty as a budding private aviator was not quite the same.

I found an Indian guy who was a story in himself. He was called Asif. He worked for Redhill Aviation Club. I originally started flying with this club, as you remember and completed the PPL written exams before going to Texas. I was looking for a low cost rental Cessna to gain experience and take all my chums up flying. I had done the required conversion Radio Telephony exam and Air Law again, to cover the differences. I had completed a night flight and some VOR tracking in Texas, *with* added spin training! All the adventures had made me more respectful of flying and I now *always* retained a healthy fear for what we were actually doing.

Redhill Aviation at the time had hired aircraft at top prices. These were very tired and I didn't know if renting these was for me again.

Asif held the way forward for me. He was an engineer who actually lived occasionally in the Southern hanger, which not many people knew about. His money was all needed for one thing and one thing only, certainly not rent. He worked as an engineer on Redhill Aviation's club aircraft. He saved enough cash to buy a low time Cessna from the States, crated it up and rebuilt it for himself, to start his *own* flying club.

What an achievement it was and a great sacrifice. I did admire him and still do, for clawing his way up from nothing. I was his first customer and watched his operation steadily grow. His aircraft was very good to fly and his engineering skills really showed. I had never flown such a tight well performing Cessna 152 ever. G-BTGR was a real peach and carried all my friends aloft. Everyone who I knew came up with me and I mean everyone.

I loved to share the experience and always remembered being ushered away as a teenager from Fairoaks Aerodrome. As a spectator some aerodrome operators in Britain don't encourage spotters and spectators alike. I had cycled from Ashtead as a teenager to Woking just to see the aircraft and been told to B~*G** off in an uncalled for way. All I was doing was *watching* the aircraft. I was the correct side of the fence and no bother to anyone. It was such a long way to ride to be told off for nothing. Funny, but later I went into Fairoaks as a pilot and was welcomed by the same guy. This is the disappointing side to aviation in Blighty.

Another problem I had seen with flying here, was the government does not pay into the aerodrome facilities so landing fees of up to £17, just to touch down the wheels are common. This with £200 per month hanger fees plus general running soon adds up. Let's not talk of fuel costs... A lack of 'experimental categories' in the CAA airworthiness system, stifle the homebuilder ambitions. Therefore homebuilding is not as common as it is in other countries. This coupled with airfields disappearing fast, to developers for housing, all has an effect of pushing up demand for aerodrome use and concentrates problems and costs. Airspace is coveted and squabbled over too, leading to noise abatement issues and local quarrels. Therefore pilots become protective and airfield operators twitchy. The costs also prohibit a certain financial class and it can seem elitist even exclusive.

I therefore was determined to welcome any spotter or interested flyer no matter what their background or income. I would obey the rules and be respectful of operator's struggles. I was going to share what I had so far and to take up people who could not afford to fly. This I did with much fun to be had. I took up Aunties, Uncles, friends' old and young, war veterans the lot. I even took up one or two who just came for a look over the fence as I had done in the past. This was great!

At the time I had several jobs to try to pay for all these '£100 per flight shots' and my money was tight, very tight. Any money I did have went up in smoke, exhaust smoke! I was being paid well at B.T. this time as a Technical Officer in London and worked at 'good old Sainsbury's' shelf stacking in the evening. At night, I even went off Minicab driving, till 1am. I started work at eight in the morning so fitting in three jobs was making me fatigued. You can only keep up this 150% working week so long, before going pop. So when I look at all my early flying photo shots, I look tired and it was no wonder. My brain and body have often been out of sync in my life. My mind wanting to do more than my body wants to. I was hungry for life and living it hard you could say.

I had no proper social life as my peers had. I did not go to clubs or the pubs with similar ages. I had no girlfriend as I was too busy. I did take a couple of girls up flying and loved their difference and was attracted to the species but often missed the important cues as I was a very busy chap.

One young girl I took up, who I did not know sat in a tandem aircraft behind and started to tickle my neck in flight asking if I liked it!

I ignored it and when we landed she was still a little flirty. But at the time, I thought she hardly knows me, so if she is like this being flirty with people she hardly knows, she would be trouble. That was not to say I did not find her attractive as she was a good looking girl. This was how it often was, when I was 23.

Going further back in time, I knew a pretty little girl called Sharon when I was 16. She was a little flirty with other boys and had other holiday boyfriends on the go. This was a secret before my twin brother found out! So, because of this I called off my affections. I was a little hurt at the time as she was because we were sweet on each other. But I always thought any courtship should lead to marriage and that was a very big important decision. She was not the girl for me. Later just before going to the States to fly, at 21years of age, I decided I would have a *real* girlfriend and court Jane properly. This was a little more serious, Jane was academic, older than me and a person we had some previous connection with as a family. She was as tall as me with brown hair cut in a 'bob.' My parents were very strict about courtship and I did follow their guidance at the time.

I courted Jane on Sunday's spending time with her family for about six months. I was always careful not to be physical and get to know the person, without the physical attraction giving a false view. She was a lovely person and when she made a move towards me with a heavy kiss, I went home thinking I must now decide to marry her. I thought I should be sure by now, having spent good time getting to know her as a person. I also wanted to fly but thought, I should *want* to save for a house instead. She went to Jersey and wanted me to come over. I did not go as I needed a chaperone and felt confused about my feelings. I called it all off and went to the US to fly. It was very sad, as I upset her deeply. I think this ability to upset someone so deeply in courtship also made me wary of any relationship with our lady friends.

My old college lecturer from Rolls Royce days, John Timms, flew a Turbulent at Redhill.

This was an old single seat design on a 'permit to fly' being a home build aircraft and the type was collected at the 'Tiger Club.' The design was cheap to run and had a VW car engine in it which was converted for aviation use. John was quite a character and a kindred spirit with a go ahead approach to life. He was tall wiry and had dark hair. He was moderately wealthy and always urged that I go and get a commercial licence. Perhaps seeing it as a chance to change my income and give me a further step up in life. He thought I would make a great airline pilot *and* I could get paid for flying.

Now aviation is effected deeply by economy and also by WW2. You see in WW2 there was a glut of pilots all of similar age. These became the pilots of BOAC and such. This then led to a 'pilot retirement wave' and replacement recruitment thereafter. Airline pilot recruitment has rippled ever since WW2. Add recession of a country and it *all* becomes about timing. My back ground being of no wealth or funds, with parents living in a council house, I would need some form of sponsorship to go commercial.

It nearly happened. I went to Gatwick and sat in the charter company Britannia's mobile recruitment van. The pilot requirement at that moment was Maths Physics at A level, 100hrs and a PPL. But a recession was looming up and the doors were shutting again. The military were also recruiting but I felt as much as I'd love the flying, that warfare is the worst thing that mankind can do. So I did not go down this route which was hard. I did therefore start A level Physics tuition privately.

This was not to be, as I became distracted with a different kind of flying. It was also very difficult with all the jobs and such, juggling everything and paying for it all. The 'commercial door' soon shut within months and then remained shut for years, on all such sponsorship schemes.

The distraction is where the fun is in the story telling and so things pick up again within this tale.

Whilst getting the chronological element right I must say John Timms and two friends used to display Turbulents. They would have the aircraft wings tied together and fly formation. They would fly low under a limbo burgee strung across the runway. Peter had a Pitts Special that he used to fly in display and I looked up to these guys as pilots. We were taught about weather being the biggest monster in swallowing up pilots and aircraft, through the C.A.A. Gasil magazines. Most accidents seem to be weather related.

These guys went home after a display into a warm front and with the cloud base lowering. They crashed all three of them, in the murky drizzle! John woke up in a ploughed field in the arms of the local vicar with a broken leg and concussion. Peter had a similar experience but had split his eye in half as well! The other guy got away with his emergency landing in another field. They were experienced clever aerobatic pilots who had pushed it to get home. Their display routine was stopped by the C.A.A. along with ever tighter display rules.

This was my first wake up call, to the reality that aviation bites and bites hard, if you do not respect it. I vowed to give it respect at all times and to respect the elements as well. It also had the effect of making me self reliant in my standing with fellow aviators. For the first time I felt a man, equal and the same when I stood next to John or any other figure in my life. Flying had finished my growing up process and helped me be decisive.

I was looking for cheaper flying at this time as well.

We had a lovely tea room at the top of Chalky's hanger. It had some old red airline fabric seats to the right, some green wicker 1920's style chairs scattered around and a WW2 parachute draped over the ceiling beams. A good pile of magazines the odd water colour of an early biplane and the compulsory tea urn and home bakes on offer. As you know I love these places and enjoyed many an afternoon chatting with fellow pilots and engineers. You could learn by listening to the chat and make important connections as well. At this time I hired Super Cubs and learnt the art of tail dragging from the proprietor Chalky. He was a tall thin chap with glasses and an easy smile. 'Tail dragging' is the art of flying aircraft with no nose wheel. It requires more rudder skill and appreciation of the angled wing in relation to the air flowing across the field. Whilst sitting on its tail wheel, the 'tail wheel aircraft' has its nose high in the air. Basically this causes, ground handling to be harder, as is takeoff and landing as well. Older aircraft are often tail draggers and it is 'key' to learn the art, if one wants to fly homebuilt and vintage aircraft.

This in a way; was my distraction from the commercial route of flying, financially it was a bad move, but it was the beginning of real fun flying.

Much later in life; in a foreign bar, I had a conversation about my flying with an older experienced 747 commercial pilot. I mentioned perhaps I should have 'gone commercial' with a little regret, holding onto my beer. He said that the type of flying I had done was the best type and that I would not have done it, or had the adventures, if I *was* commercial. In some ways he was right, as at this time I would have been instrument training at Biggin Hill. No way as carefree as tail dragging was with Chalky.

There was a conversation had in Chalky's tea room, with some old chaps who were *building* a tail dragger. These guys were slightly laughed at, for dreaming the dream of homebuilding and buying a kit from another country. It was not common in Blighty to build one's own plane and fly it at the time. Yes it happened, but not like in the USA. It represented about eight percent of the aircraft flying around. What it offered was, affordable flying and group ownership. What it did not offer was an aircraft that had been tested for years. See every Cessna or Piper is a very proven design with every aspect of operation and maintenance sorted out to a high standard. The aircraft were over engineered to a ratio of seven times, on the whole. Every vintage aircraft too had a similar history of design and maintenance evolution that made them safe as machines. This often left only the pilot as the weakest link to flight safety. These home brews were kits from the USA designed in experimental category shipped to Blighty and set in a 'Permit to fly' category via the PFA.

The Popular Flying Association was the link between the C.A.A. and all the 'red tape' and approved certain designs as safe to build. It helped with creating safe practices and a host of other things for home build projects. (It still does today under a different name now the LAA)

The Kitfox Mk2 was an exciting tale, what happened is well worth writing about.

These four older chaps were busy building this splendid looking USA designed Kitfox Mk2 kit in their garage back home. I was in need of some cheap flying to be able to go back to doing one secular job and have a sustainable means of getting aloft. I decided in the tea room to buy into a quarter share of the unfinished project and to help finish it off. The idea was enticing. You see this aircraft had folding wings; it was also being built right near Redhill Aerodrome. We could hanger it in the garage, fold the wings, drive it to the

aerodrome all of 800 yards, unfold the wings and beat hanger fees. Maintenance would be done by us and signed off by a qualified engineer.

Most of these practices did work and come about only it was awful wide when towing behind a car! Thank goodness we garaged it a few yards away. Also the other cracks that started to appear were in design and lack of proving by the manufacturer. More on this, later: Fun wise it had loads to get enthusiastic about. The guys were amazing chaps that had lived a thousand lives. These were the kind of guys, that it is good to yarn in the pub with, over a good pint of British ale. They had ridden motorbikes when all was very unsafe and unreliable. They had been motor racing in times gone by and flown when there were hardly any rules. George had a wooden leg as he lost one leg in a motorcycle accident. Years ago he had landed a Miles Majister right near Wandsworth prison having run out of fuel! They were different to guys we had known in my family and stimulating to be around.

I was lucky to be accepted in the group and lucky to have a 'quarter share' in their hard work so far. The Kitfox was full of paper problems in the respect to the PFA and CAA. She was however a lovely aeroplane to look at and sit in. She was yellow and red with a lovely round cowling at the front. It had a high wing, with side by side seating and an old 1940's look about it. It was a kit from the U.S.A. invented by Dan Denny. The seats had four point harnesses and were comfortable. It was light being built with a complex steel tube fuselage covered in fabric. When I sat in it, I thought 'a spill' on takeoff could well be survivable even quite safe. Such was the clever construction. I was beginning to pick up that; fast heavy aeroplanes with poor restraint like Piper and some Cessna's could be lethal, should impact occur. This aircraft seemed safe by way of a good impact absorbing structure and the crucial four point harnesses.

G-BSAZ Kitfox Mk2 was getting ready for flight. I remember sitting in the drive, adding some more 'running in time' to the engine, setting different throttle settings to help bed it in. We needed 12 hours ground running, much to the annoyance of the direct neighbours who were very surprised to see a full size aeroplane running up in the drive! I loved it, seeing pansies flying around and cats running off. Bizarre was fun at the time and this was all bizarre.

Paper work bogged us down and a slight chill ran through us all. By the time we had built our lovely aeroplane, early Kitfox Mk2's were crashing! Dan Denny had sold the company and the engine manufacturer Rotax wrote to try to say, the engine was not fit for flight! This was yet *another* worry for the group.

I flew into Rochester in another aeroplane and was talking to some chaps about the Kitfox and this Army Helicopter pilot came over, seeking me out. He was on crutches and was adamant that I did not fly the Kitfox. The last thing he saw was blades of grass just before impact! He took off in *his* new Mk2 with his dad watching and 'tip stalled' to spin in at a height of 800ft. "Don't fly it!" he said in a concerned forceful way that sent a chill up my spine. See this guy must be an experienced flyer, coming from the forces, I thought. It did however confirm my suspicion that it was a forgiving design to hit the floor with!

Well we *did* end up flying it, because of much research and because of some ignorance or desperation. George with the wooden leg flew it and so did I. The other two group members were eventually excluded because the insurance company stated that; only pilots, who *had* flown it, could fly it. By this time twelve had crashed and I was wary of the new yellow beastie. It was hot news amongst fellow aviators at the time.

I met a guy called Martin Pettifer. He was one pilot like me in that he wanted to fly for fun, share it and fly interesting stuff.

Martin and I were of similar spirits, we loved flight and we loved planes. We both were not wealthy and of similar incomes. He was a little older and drove a red Mini which had so many plates of metal welded on it was a heavy sculpture in its own right. He was *as* tall as me with brown hair and a small scar on his face from a bad cycle crash. We loved vintage aircraft and the freedom of the past ways in flying. Open cockpit called us both, but we had not done it yet. Martin was an Ab-initio instructor and was currently flying a shabby Condor dishing out flights to anyone interested and helping out with tail dragging tuition. This aircraft was run on a shoe string by a chap called Mike Pier who owed people money and had a strange group share set up to pay for it. The aircraft airframe was great, but the engine was serviced on budget and the canopy needed replacing as did the interior. Martin was an intrepid adventurer in light aviation and went everywhere. He was less of a worrier than me and more experience and even went to Ireland in the Condor. He went all over and was gaining valuable experience all the time.

Enter the Kitfox into the story and I'll explain the funny side at the end.

Now I asked my brother Grant to come and fly it with me as the crashes all seemed to be pilot error. Grant was also an adventure loving maverick and would not mind the odd bump. Being my older brother who was very familiar, my concentration would be on the aircraft and not on my passenger. So my first proper solo flight in the Kitfox MK2 was with Grant and I tested it to the full, perfecting the flare in the landing which seemed to 'get' most Kitfox pilots at the time. Also on takeoff the thing could bite, I knew this first hand from Rochester, don't forget. My confidence grew with the little beastie that looked so innocent; at least it had good seat belts I thought.

The design was flawed in several ways. Let me explain. The wing was huge with curled tips to hold in lift at slow speed. It was designed as a STOL aircraft. (Short take off and landing) It had a low power to weight ratio with big wings. Trouble is; with a low wing loading, one needs big control surfaces because the airflow can be slow at times. Control is equal to force over the area so *if* it is slow it needs big paddles to steer. The keel, or length from wing to tail, was quite small. This distance to the tail is also the leverage force needed for control. The keel on the Kitfox being small was another reason to have a larger rudder and elevators. It had a small elevator and rudder *and* a small keel as well! (See with these things it is either or preferably both.)

The Kitfox Mk2 wing started flying at 30mph. The Ailerons (for roll control) were flaperons or flaps as well. So the PFA decreed, in their involvement. Dan Denny the designer said 'they controlled pitch in flight and trimmed the plane.' I favoured his thoughts but the PFA made us put a trim tab on the back elevator and use them as flaps. This compounded a problem as now, the wing with full flap on approach, stalled at *less* than 30mph. The trouble was the controls gave up proper response around 40mph!

On takeoff there was a bad spot of 'little control' initially, but it was better with the prop draft. On landing in the flare at say 35mph it gave little or no control the throttle being closed, 'it was horrible.' I didn't use the flaperons as flaps and left them at zero degrees for each flight. I ended up, leaving a slight crack of power on when landing and dragged the brakes. This gave me more control over the back end. This is so hard, as you don't want to flip it over being a tail dragger. On takeoff it was; tail up ASAP and hold it down with pitch till control was sure. Don't let it climb too steep even though it wanted to do just that. I remembered our friend at Rochester with every climb out. It was best to fly *not* in STOL configuration at all.

Twelve had crashed and the group was falling out over whether to sell it or not. No one wanted Kitfox right now so a massive loss was being hotly debated. It cost £18,000 and took four years to build. I for my part kept out of the heavy discussions and was saddened to see lifelong friends fall out over something material. George was going to fly it and could not understand the hot air or the CAA. He had no fear and was stuck in the past in his views of 'unnecessary paper work from the CAA.' It *was* serious and it was lucky no one had died at this point in the Kitfox mk2's history. It was however proving very forgiving in a 'crump.'

We did have a problem with vibration at this point. In shutting it down, it gave a shudder on the last engine note when stopping. I heard a 'click' from the tube welded airframe one day and the weld joint holding the rpm gauge to the fuselage, cracked. I took advice and was told vibration exits a structure and can crack things at its exit point. This alarmed me and made more arguments in the group. I thought; 'where will the vibration exit on the next shut down? Can we always see where the damage is? Will it be an important part of the airframe?' I was not happy to fly it, till this was resolved.

It was resolved by Rotax when a guy was flying a Rans S10 midwing kit built aeroplane which had the same B type metalstic gearbox bush. His RPM gauge shot up over Kent and he pulled the throttle shut in mid cruise. As he did the Propeller flew off! He said 'It was like one of those toys we had, that you pull the cord and the plastic prop disc flies off the hand held drive!' Needless to say he had an engine failure; well prop disappearance actually. He landed safely in a field. He never found the prop, but it would be a great thought, to think it ended up in someone's garden un- announced and the person treasured their finding. After all, props can fetch good money as decorative items.

Rotax changed the gearbox to a new C type and I flew the Kitfox again this time with Martin, this is the funny bit.

I felt the future of the Kitfox was not in the group and they did not like me or George flying it as we might well crash it. The other two members were trying to flog it off. I put it to Martin 'perhaps us two could buy it cheap and fly it together.' I asked for his experience to come and assess the aircraft in its handling and would advertise my idea to him, thereby saving the yellow beastie.

As we took off, for Headcorn in Kent, a friendly grass strip Martin watched and smiled through his round Harry Potter style glasses. These were distinct and trendy at the time most people's glasses being rectangle with the fashion. I made a complete fool of myself as the aircraft had a 'preset flip flop Radio.' You could set the next leg frequency up in on the LED screen and talk on the other. I did not understand the flip over sequence. Leaving Redhill zone after my takeoff; I called up Redhill by mistake, in trying to call up Headcorn! I then did it again saying to Martin and all the aircraft at the time in the circuit "What a Plonker!" I was saying this about myself but transmitted it out onto the frequency in my fluster. I was embarrassed as I had advertised the benefits of this Radio; as part of my sales campaign to Martin. Now it was causing me problems. I knew Martin only briefly before and so was more self conscious than I would have been. Get this, I did it a third time and only then understood the radios operation. I was quick to get off Redhill's airways! Martin was killing himself laughing and my red face eased as I realised the funny side. It did break the ice between us and we got stuck into handling the aircraft and thoroughly air testing it.

When you test an aircraft like this, there are no real manuals of test and it is all feel. Basic airmanship becomes very important and also a will to push it, feel, learn, and fully understand. It is very interesting and we became lost in it all, fighting to understand what made this tricky to land and why so many had crashed. It was perfect weather this day which helped us in our quest.

We stalled it with power on; level, nose high with it off and side slipped it for good measure. Flaperons up and down all landing combinations possible were tested. We were so lost in the testing we ate the fuel up and we had about 10mins flight duration left on the downwind leg to Headcorn. It was a balmy summer's day and the airfield and radio was very busy. I said to Martin to 'give it a go and land the thing, I'll do the radio.'

I remember him pulling himself up in the seat and breathing in, in an older wiser big brother way. He was thinking; 'I'll show him how it should be done, I'll grease it in.' Full of confidence in his ability, he performed a conventional approach. I was a little puzzled by this and slightly worried but bowed to his experience. Well, it did the 'Kitfox Mk2 scary buck' on touchdown. As the tail lowered it bounced high into the air, with a high angle of attack and 'with nothing on the clocks but the makers' name! (Or stall) It was very violent and unless quickly caught with full power stick forward; it could be bad, very bad! Martin was deeply shocked. No longer was he relaxed and sure I could see this with the new tension as he caught it. I trusted he would catch it well and on time. I sat back in the seat.

We climbed away me calling "Golf Alpha Zulu, going around." On the 'flip flop' radio. I was glad Martin could now see she was different and asked him, now he was focused, if he could come up with something else? His experience led him to try a different higher STOL approach. After all the aircraft was originally sold for short take off and landing. In we came again on finals for Headcorn. The words 'Kitfox' back then were exciting to one and all as there was a big question mark over it. It was in hot debate in club houses and I noticed a small crowd of spotters and spectators gathering outside the club house on approach. I also wondered who was listening on the radio to the words 'Kitfox.'

Headcorn was unique as owner operator Peter was in a wheel chair and was very open to spotters and general public using the airfield for fun. There was a Museum of sorts, a great tea room open to all public and it had a landing fee of £2! This guy was not the norm and was famous for his hospitality and free thinking. The ramp area and tea room was open to spotters and everyone, it was always crowded.

We slid down the final approach with quite a high descent rate building up. It built up so fast, which again alarmed Martin. He wrestled it and set up a text book STOL landing just in time. BANG! We bounced in so hard I thought the wings were going to break! Boing! Up we shot Martin caught it and I radioed "Golf Alpha Zulu, going around" off we went *again.* I looked at the fuel and it said empty pretty much. Martin looked and then we looked at each other. We were not pilots at this point, we were not men. We were 12 year old boys who climbed a tree with great bravado and could not now get down!

Anyone who was anyone in the light aviation scene well knew that the Kitfox Mk2 was iffy. People down in the club house who were curious; 'would *they* now see another crash?' The spotters and such on the ground would have a tale to tell and I would be in trouble with the other group members for bending it. These were the thoughts running through my mind.

What was great though, was Martin and I had bonded in a way that only this situation brings. He used this tale at his wedding dinner table for peat sake. Yes it was a real tale and here is how it ended.

I suddenly remembered dragging the brakes slightly and landing quite well with Grant, so this was the only way albeit a tad dangerous. So I set it up on finals and landed the 'beastie.' It took every fibre of my body in concentration, wanting the outcome to be a good one. The thoughts of embarrassment with some form of 'pilot error' and bending the Kitfox close in mind. Oddly self preservation did not come into it. Being young, danger to us did not feature much in our own minds or perhaps we had no time to reflect. When we taxied back, our relief turned to confidence and we started to feel good about the whole experience, bar a tad embarrassed with all the bouncing landing attempts.

I started my sales pitch up again, about us forming a group together, as we taxied to a stop. But when we alighted I suddenly saw the damage to the Kitfox rudder! The thought of the guys telling me off was first in my mind and the group quarrelling again. They had let me fly it on deep trust and I dare not damage it, it was so shiny and new. Picture this, I was in full sales patter when suddenly, I dived to the floor by the tail, trying to pull the dented rudder straight again. I was shouting "Nooooooo!" The contrast from the sales patter was so great it made Martin almost cry with laughter to watch me. The tail wheel had bashed several times right into the rudder on the monstrous bounds back into air, whilst 'going around.'

Martin eventually talked me down and we had tea and a chocolate cookie in the club house. I could not be too consoled, as I knew the Kitfox and my first share in an aeroplane was doomed. Martin was not going to come up with a rescue plan and it was flawed by design.

We flew the Kitfox home Martin landed similar to me; back at Redhill, only it was a greaser. I paid for the rudder to be fixed, with Chalky's engineers.

The wind worried me this day and so did George.

Dan Air had gone bust at this time and Mark wanted to go to Southend airport to see the old aircraft from the company. I was ordered by George to get the Kitfox out the southern hanger. The wind was about 30kts and most aircraft were not operating. I had said to George not to fly the Kitfox as the wind was too high for this type of aircraft. He was having none of it. Under slight pressure I taxied out to prepare it for flight for George filling it with fuel etc. As I taxied around the starboard wing lifted up with me in it at rest the engine ticking over. I kicked it 'dead into wind' held in full up to hold the tail down and added a blast of power. I managed to taxi to a sheltered part of the aerodrome by dragging the brakes with some throttle open. I warned George of the wind strength and he said I worried too much. He promptly got in it and took off for Headcorn. Looking back probably their combined weight made it all ok, just, but I was now worrying about him.

With all this in mind I selected Chalky's super Cub for hire to take Mark up, reasoning the extra weight was better in the brisk wind. The Super Cub was heavier by design, but it was still a taildragger and so hard to operate in heavy wind. I wanted to go to Headcorn, as a grass runway is more forgiving in a cross wind. Mark insisted on Southend to see the old Dan Air jets. Off we went with my mind still on George and the Kitfox. I was soon in focus again as the wind was a battle on finals to Southend. I pulled off a cracking landing and relaxed. Now; it is not over till you walk away, with flying aeroplanes and only then can you relax. I parked on the apron and looked for some chocks in the back luggage compartment. Chalky had none in his Cub for fear of loose items getting caught up in the back end of the fuselage. I put the hydraulic brakes on tight and gave the Cub a tug when we had alighted. It felt ok to leave it and look for some chocks around the ramp area. This Southend airport was a more commercial operation and I could not find any 'for the love of me.' I gave the Cub another tug to make sure it was not going to move and followed an inpatient Mark into the posh viewing area. This viewing area was a Café and seating place with a splendid view of the ramp and runway. It was packed this day, as most pilots were not flying due to the high wind. Mark ordered bacon sarnies and coffees for us and he was happy.

As I sipped my coffee slowly relaxing, I spotted our Super Cub parked up *but* moving backwards! I had to do a double take; yes it was inching backwards and moving faster now. An aircraft in front was performing an engine run up test and had blown our Cub backwards. I threw my coffee down and raced to the ramp. Shouthend airport had a customs area and it took valuable seconds to dive over the desks and explain my actions to security staff. As I appeared back on the ramp, our Cub had gathered momentum travelling backwards and smashed into a Bandeirante commercial aeroplane! The tower had hit the red emergency button and a fire engine was at the scene quick as a flash. I was wearing a flying suit and was so embarrassed walking over to the Cub. I was mobbed by local engineers with offers to repair her. The Rudder was bashed in and the most obvious visible damage. The aileron was dented slightly and she had a brake leak, which I found out later on. I knew Chalky was hard up for business cash right now and would like his team to repair it through his insurance.

I taxied it back to where it was originally parked. The commercial aeroplane only had a slightly dented propeller spinner. This aircraft was soon deemed 'fit to fly' and later took off with the evening mail or some such cargo. The company did not insist on the spinner to be repaired and just accepted it.

I filled out the AIB (Accident Information Bureau) forms which was slightly humiliating as I never thought I would have to fill one of these out in all my flying. I was informed that this was how the Gasil magazine published information, by viewing these forms. I tried to telephone Chalky at the time but was unable to get an answer. Time past and I hatched a plan to taxi the Cub over to the other side, to park it up for a few days.

One thing a pilot gets to do is to check out his 'chosen mount' prior to using it. This is called the 'walk round check.' A good pilot will always do this, checking every component of the airframe before *every* flight sector. I performed no walk round, as I was only going to taxi to the other side. I knew it was not fit for flight. Mark and I climbed straight back into the Cub and fired it up. You can only imagine the embarrassment as a fresh set of pilots in the viewing area, now banged on the glass, pointing to the back of the Cub. I could see them shouting "look at the back of the plane!" in great animation and concern for us. I taxied off trying not to look at them as explanation would only take *more* time.

So now at the other side of the airport I met an engineer and asked for some long nose pliers. I removed the rudder and hired a taxi. We paid the £70 and asked the driver to get us back to Redhill quick. It was hard getting in his car with the Cub rudder as well but we managed. When we arrived at Redhill you should have seen chalky's face. He was locking up and worrying where we were as it was getting dark. I dived out the taxi clutching the rudder of his precious Cub. "You know the Cub we hired from you...?" You can imagine his reaction!

on the engine mount bolts I tried to wriggle out. Somehow I was stuck and it was the last straw.

I cried and cried. I could hear myself cry! I was all alone, in a field stuck upside down in my little ship trying and trying to wiggle free. The instrument panel was cutting my back but it was *all* the trying, that came to a head. After I had cried I felt better, relaxed and wriggled free it was a turning point.

When my VP1 was finished, she sported independent Morris Marina master brake cylinders, with Go Cart calliper and discs, giving great stopping and turning ability. She had a super zero timed engine, radio and bespoke rudder hinges an improvement on the original design. This was hard to get through the PFA improvement system as any new changes to design is met with 'you can't do that, unless it is approved.' "How do you get approval?" I would ask. Blah! Blah! And we would arrive at a full stop in conversation. Arrrhhhh! It was so frustrating, how hard it was, to make it happen. It was nothing like building a car or boat.

It was not too soon that I was doing the preverbal 'running in' of the engine with the twelve ground hours required. I taxied round to start with but soon started to tie the tail to a fence post, setting the throttle and doing other jobs like servicing my car. I often wondered what it would be like if the knot came undone and she flew away with me chasing it, no one on board! I told you the mind wanders; I was back to my old self after 'the big cry.'

Before my first ever flight in the Evans VP1; the signing off engineer, broke my Pitot tube the evening before. He used araldite to glue it back on, blocking it up as the glue ran back inside and hardened off.

Incidentally the way it works with Permit maintenance is the CAA through the PFA requires two engineers to sign the thing off, fit to fly. The owner can be one of the engineers in this process if the qualified guy is happy with his work, he being the final check on everything and legally responsible. There is a Propeller log, an airframe log and an engine log...

On my first ever take off in a single seat homebuilt aircraft following this final signing; I charged up the strip, to a tree line in Truleigh farm near Fulking Sussex.

I had no choice in the direction of takeoff on this day, downhill being down wind. The rudder was sensitive as it was an all flying design; not being used to it I started an oscillating yaw in the VP1. With single seat aircraft no one can teach you to fly it, you have to get in it and get used to it quickly. I realised I was overcorrecting and dampened my movements, but precious seconds ticked by. Then when I looked at the airspeed indicator it read Zero! An Airspeed indicator is a good primary instrument to have on your first flight. I looked at the trees and I was just un-sticking from the ground. By this time, the hedge looming up was an issue for stopping. Now I had spent so long fettling it, I was not going try to stop only to damage her in the hedge which was too near at this point. So I went for it! I elected to fly with no Airspeed instrument and save the VP1, not ideal.

As I arose, I kept the same wind speed on my face and made sure the climb was shallow with no turns. I was fully aware of not knowing the aircraft in feel and having no ASI, that it was only 'good old airmanship' that would save me. It was the stuff that the early pioneers were doing long before fancy instrument aids, crept over cockpit panels. At about 700ft I made my first very awkward turn. See the ailerons gave slight adverse yaw and needed rudder to work well, but the rudder took some getting used to it being all flying and very sensitive. The seat belt was second hand, an ex RAF glider snap shut type, but it was worn. I was unaware it had worked undone in my takeoff. As the VP1 skidded in this first turn I almost fell out! Unnerving to say the least, but through all this, the cold shocking air forced down ones lungs wakes you up! I must have had some adrenaline flowing through these cold veins I'm sure.

I remember skimming the South Downs and a couple were walking their black Labrador dog. I saw them looking up at me wondering perhaps; why I was close. It was quite a sight but as I was close to the hill it was not surreal like flying above 500ft or so. No this was like being up a ladder and it felt high looking down at these dog walkers. Perhaps it was the lack of cockpit to cocoon, but VP1 flying, *really* felt like flying. I was not normally in the habit of low flying; it was just a ragged heading.

When I had levelled off and realised that I could do this flight safely, I relaxed for the first time in the VP1. It was at that moment that one tends to feel it is all worth it, to see life in such another way. Open cockpit gives you a feeling for the air you are in. You literally feel every airspeed change on your face. You can smell the sea or bonfire you fly over. You can feel the damp of a cloud and its cold, bursting out into the warmth of the sun the other side. Crystal views, not looking through yellowing scratched Perspex. No vinyl interior and petrol sickly smell from an old 'spam can' Cessna style. The wide fresh view of open cockpit, made it all suddenly worth it. Exciting and beautiful; but I did need to still concentrate if I was going to get it together, on this first flight.

I stalled it deliberately at 1000ft to see the effect of the wind on my face and it was slight. So I had been 'well in' on speed all this time, phew! The other instruments were checked and worked well. This is a worthy check when flying a test flight to see what you have to work with. I did a few turns to work out the required rudder aileron mix to give better balanced turns, my seat belt annoyingly popping undone from time to time. I was south of Gatwick control zone and now looking for my map.

I had flown 'open cockpit' once only in a Stampe SV4 prior to all this. I was told to have a 250mil map in my boot as a spare and 500mil on my knee clip. Which I did, but it was folded in the wrong place which was a small unknown error in my part. In attempting to unfold the map, the crazy torso turbulence; unique to VP1 flying, ripped it clean out my hand! I glanced back and gained a sense of speed in my aerial world as it opened out floating below and behind. Wow! Still I had my trusty 250 map in my boot. Then Blast! Exactly the same thing happened again. It ripped clean out my hand, gone! These were about £8 each at the time and semi precious to me. I made a half turn to watch it fall below. The half thought did occur to dive back down, fly under and to catch it. But I had enough on my plate and the prop could catch it and get damaged, so my attention turned to making contact on my new radio. This had been set to Shoreham and Gatwick pre flight.

Now this Radio was an expensive Icom with a VOR function for radio tracking. It was hand held but mounted on the instrument panel on a special clip. The aerial cable went from the front to a ground plate and aerial at the rear. There was a connector that enabled me to take it out on away visits and in storage, to save it being stolen. As I saddled up for this first flight I unwittingly sat on the coaxial connector. It was on and transmitting but not out through the aerial so it was no use at all.

This took a few minutes to work out and was not easy as it sounds. The aircraft went into a shallow right hand climbing turn when you let the controls go. Trim tabs had not been added prior as it is the sort of thing that gets done well after the flight test and proper evaluation of the cruise. Things were starting to list up in this first flight. No radio no maps, no airspeed indicator, a dickey seat belt and *all* on the first flight. The outcome was dependant on thought and discipline, in other words basic airmanship.

I used to receive 'Gasil,' (General Aviation Safety Information Leaflet) monthly incident and accident magazine by the CAA giving all the info on crashes. They printed the events before a crash and all the 'incidents' that lead to the accident. It is always several small problems that added up to the big smash. Many readers thought; whilst reading, 'well I would not do that,' in a confident, almost arrogant way. It was intended to sow a seed in learning from others mistakes. At best the reader would remember not to fly in bad weather or check this or that, so that calamity could be avoided.

But right here; now, in my boots, if the AIB investigated my crash and 'Gasil' printed it, people would say 'what was he doing flying with no airspeed indicator!' Or 'I would never fly with a faulty radio or without a map! I could now see how these incidents started to add up and realised I was still in some danger and would have to concentrate all the way, lest something else should happen. It later made me read with understanding and humility my monthly Gasil magazine!

It was at that moment that I became determined to *make it happen*. I knew the air layout of zones etc. and had a good map in my head of the south of England. As long as I went to Hazlemere and kept below 1500ft. Then turned North, then followed the railway West, I would see Redhill aerodrome on my nose.

All went well and I slowly relaxed a little again. Cruising along, with the railway line to my left, I was enjoying the fresh air and uninterrupted view that only a VP1 can give. At around 1500ft the air is cleaner and very refreshing. At a constant height above sea one can see hills you never knew existed and it feels privileged to view it all open cockpit, just as the early aviators did. The feeling also; that this was my baby too, a new feeling that I owned this one. It was the first time I had owned an aircraft whole, no club hassling for its return. I could go somewhere for the day and visit the local town say; or even stay over. The thoughts of total freedom were grand. It was a feeling that capitalised what it was that made me do it; fly I mean. I flew for the view, the freedom and the fresh air to feel alive really alive. Commercial flying thoughts were slipping a tad; right at this point I was officially distracted.

Nearing Redhill the tension returned my dream world was real again, very real. Redhill aerodrome was a helicopter training ground for Bristow Helicopters. The year previous a Cherokee or some low wing 'spam can' had crashed, with the vortex ring of air a helicopter had created in the hover, next to the active runway. The controllers were tense and particular about all movements. In some way authoritarian, this later caused its own problems. Phil was on duty today and his voice was intimidating in some way. He would sometimes be sarcastic on the radio in tone and tell people off. He was often right but it is better kept off the airways and not very professional. Redhill was making a transition from club field to Bristows Airport.

The 'no radio light signals procedures' were read about, but never really applied by pilots and controllers as most people had radios. Those very rare aircraft that did not have radios, the pilots would telephone prior to arriving giving a landing time. The controller could then look out in advance and be ready with light signals.

So I joined overhead the circuit as strict procedure for 'no radio working,' but was unnoticed totally! Typical; on finals I watched for lights and saw none. Fly the plane then communicate, but above all fly the plane I thought. I set myself up on approach having done what I was supposed to and checked for light signals which never came. I flew in fast deliberately; to avoid stalling and this made my elevator lively. It was sensitive anyway but now it was pitchy as hell. But I was not going to stall. My plan was dive for the runway numbers, flare out level and then with the throttle shut, feel for the ground. When the aircraft wanted to stop flying it would and I would be inches above the ground. 'Try to keep flying it will give up when the speed runs out' I thought. It all worked a treat; I achieved a three pointer eating up most of the runway mind, as my speed over the numbers was very high. I also reduced the throttle slowly to dampen torque effecting yaw, which contributed to distance on the runway. 'Better safe than sorry.'

I remember going over to the tower pulling my flying helmet off and noticing for the first time the sweat I had made. It was not warm in the VP1 but I was dripping under my flying helmet, curious. It was all the tension of 'flying by the seat of your pants.' What relief I now felt and my confidence crept up a smidge. The faults could be all fixed. I had my ship, which was owned solely by me. A sense of pride and achievement came over me, I had learnt a lot. Phil was not as concerned as he should have been, he did not see me on my arrival or seem bothered. I was not one for confrontation and if he was happy I was out of there. I left the tower to taxi over to see Chalky and my fellow club mates, to show off my new toy. No one seemed impressed with it as a machine but week smiles told me they thought a little more of the achievement as a whole. After all, I was alive!

Later in the day, time whooshed and after lots of chat and tea in the club house I started to feel my old self again only now with a story to share. The weather started to come in; it was not forecast this

Cumulus Nimbus. "Better get that in the southern hanger Lloyd, it's going to rain," Chalky said. So I started to fix the connector to the radio prompt, as this aerodrome was controlled airspace even to taxi around on. I leapt into the VP1 to taxi to the Southern hanger, which was quite a way over the other side. As I waited for taxi clearance; the radio now fixed and working well, the Cumulus Nimbus opened up with heavy rain!

This was so open cockpit, that I looked very wet before I even started off. I could see the chaps laughing at me a sorry figure quite un-protected. Now serious Phil who did things all proper did something most odd and out of character. He used the airways to laugh! It was a deep Huh! Huh! Huh! No one could transmit or hear a thing only him laughing at me sitting in the open VP1 in the rain. To be honest it did break my tension and made me laugh too. Back in the southern hanger I think it was me who truly had the last laugh though, as all the adventure was to come from my little VP1.There was nothing quite like the extreme open cockpit of my little ship.

B.T. was to offer redundancy and at the time I had achieved all there was to achieve in the company.

It was only going to be more of the same; some birds are not meant to be caged. When the lump sum came all I could think was, 'let's go flying!' Looking back I could have invested it in property or such and had more money now; but in some way 'life is for living' and whilst one is young, it is a time free from health issues on the whole. So at the time I chose to live and blew the lot flying. I look at my log book now and think of the memories, not the thousands wasted which is somewhat fortunate.

The commercial window was closing and I thought I best give it another stab to see if this was for me and if I could break through into a world of being paid to fly. I organised; in a fashion not dissimilar to my work experience as a lad, to get B.T. to pay for some more flying. This flying was 're-deployment training.'

I knew this flying club in Biggin Hill operated twin engine aircraft. As commercial was all about instruments and multi engines, I thought it was a good place to see if commercial was really for me.

B.T. was offering training at the time, as well as the redundancy. An additional package that helped with training, so that employment after redundancy was possible for its staff. Not many knew about it and there was an upper cash limit. This upper limit was the exact fee for the Multi Engine group B test. I had to get the club to fax the information over and fill out some forms. Months after my leaving I was surprised and delighted that the club had received a cheque from B.T. 'Let's go flying twin engines,' I thought. And so I ended up doing a twin rating at Biggin Hill thanks to B.T... This was fun and very different flying.

No time to have a little dream or stare at the view, for a moment.

The Grumman Cougar had GA7 shot off like a scalded cat and had many systems to look after. This was the aircraft I rented to learn twin engine flying.

G-PLAS GRUMMAN COUGAR GA7

It was compounding in that as one travelled faster the radio and navigation came up quicker as well. I felt like a 'one armed paper hanger,' as they say. It flew on rails and was equipped with luxuries like electric trims and such. I was fascinated that the "poling" or hand work on the yolk was so little. It knew where it was supposed to go. So this was all about numbers check lists and perfecting drills. Manifold pressure, prop pitch, rpm, and blue line speed etc. It did feel great having all that thrust on takeoff, a sense of power like driving a powerful car, only better.

I only found the handling entertaining with the engine out one side. Or, 'dead stick on one.' The aircraft needs to be balanced with rudder which is fine till the speed on approach starts changing. Then it all feels squirmy and odd. See the rudder is as good as the airflow over it, so as speed changes, so does rudder effectiveness. Engine out landings were a challenge and I remember getting a bit near a lorry on approach near Le Touquet in France. Yes France, this thing flew well and a quick flip over the channel for lunch was 45 minutes away. Speed and distance were a bonus to such twin engine aircraft and they are safer over water.

A lovely memory was had seeing small cumulus cloud tops orange, by the setting sun. We were skimming over these puffy clouds fast with the sea below. It was a feeling of speed and beauty looking down the channel that evening.

The instructor knew I was not financially committed to commercial flying and that I flew a homebuilt aircraft. I think he thought I was some kind of maverick flyer which was far from the truth, he viewed my training as a fun day out and let me have full reign. The recession had hit the country, this was 1992 and the club was quiet. The instructor was earning about £20 per day and times were hard. The order of the day was; we did some heavy drilling in the classroom, but the flying was a 'fun lesson.' I think the commercial courses were all about deadlines and money. These were stressful for student and instructor in the main. We both had fun on G-PLAS and it was refreshing landing somewhere new and fit for purpose in every way.

It was here and now that I assessed the commercial route and made a conscious choice. The recession was on, my timing was off and those who were braving it were getting head over heels in debt. I knew several guys, who ended up remortgaging their homes to keep licences going, with no hope of a job. I was not going to get into debt the same. Also I started to realise what I liked about flying as I drove back down from 'Biggin on the bump.' The twin had given me a slight headache literally. Yes it was a challenge but that was all. The

VP1 however was freedom views and much more. You felt like a time traveller in it and could know what the early aviators felt. If you don't look at a road, who is to say, you were not in 1930's?

I had a job selling tickets on British rail and having always spent every penny had no spare cash only my wages at the end. I went back to my default and did nothing further towards the commercial route. My default was; to seek out the staff on the railway, the platform sweepers and such and take them for an aerial ride. I hired a Jodel or Super cub and went on the lookout for kindred spirits to share in the fun. With the VP1 hangerage and such, I could only afford say one flight a month rental. With the VP1 costs paid for there was only the fuel to add, so I flew this more at this time.

As funds were tight I drove a 2CV but this soon became a Lomax 223 with many modifications. This was a small open cockpit two seat sports car. It was a front wheel drive three wheeler with one wheel at the back using the 2CV engine and chassis. It was a great car that gave me the feeling of being open cockpit like my VP1. It had no roof and was of a 1930's styling with two little aero screens. When it rained I only became wet below 35mph as the airflow around the body kept the water off me. I kept a 'golfing brolley' in it to put up, if I was stuck in traffic. I was working at Dorking station at the time and owned the car for a year. Sometimes I would see the first train leave Ashtead bound for Dorking and it would be my first duty to open up on its arrival in the morning. I would race this train to work. The train would have to stop at Leatherhead and so I had half a chance to beat it. I would go flat out and the Lomax handled great.
This great handling was later to work against me in similar car, later on in life.
Now though was a great time in life, I was happy free and living with adventure daily. There were no girls in my life but this was soon to change.

One last VP1 story; as I could go on and on about every flight.

Martin was flying the Condor and we decided to go to a BBQ fly in at LEC refrigeration Bognor Regis. Yes the owner of LEC had a small downhill concrete strip right near the A27. There was a bit of clag (low cloud) hanging around and we managed to snuck through. We were to be in formation flight and I said to Martin that; 'if we should pop in cloud, that he should open up his throttle which would move him forward.' We were VFR (Visual Flight Rules) machines and had no intention of messing in cloud without the proper instruments and so he said to me, 'steer well clear of any fluffy stuff.' We had great fun taking shots with our film cameras not knowing what we had in the bag, as photography was back then. I was navigating and Martin was in loose formation.

A small stray cumulus blob appeared too high and low for me to avoid and we both popped in it, in close formation. I sat there for a second hoping not to do a 180 degree turn and fly back out as it was all going to plan navigation wise. Sure enough it was a stray puff and I popped out again very soon. Martin; to my astonishment, was slap bang on my wing tip! He had not moved his throttle open; thank goodness we had not bumped into each other.

We landed full of smiles and I met the engineer Andy who signed off the VP1. A great day was had by all and so it was, this flying gave a little adventure every time.

Oh! I'll squash one more last story in.

The only hard flight I had in the VP1 was going to Old Sarum in the depths of winter. 22/12/1992 was the exact date and 'blimming cold,' about two degrees Celsius static. Airborne you have three degrees per thousand feet drop in temperature and prop draft from the propeller adds to effect. The old WW2 style flying jacket kept most of the extreme cold out, but you are just sitting still taking it.

I had two military jets come to see me in MATZ airspace. (Military Air Traffic Zone) One was flying upside down over the top of me. The other was in mirror formation the right way round going underneath. I was praying the jet wash did not upset the air I was in and send me tumbling. It was great for them but not for me. I saw a cockpit flash from the one on top and swear he took a photo of me.

When I got to Old Sarum and lined up on finals to land, I was so cold, I could barely move. I could not talk at all on the radio to announce my arrival to the tower. I was thankful the air was still, as any bumps would have seen me crash on the runway as I was frozen solid. My movement on the controls had slowed right down and you do need to be brisk sometimes when landing low and slow. When I stopped, I felt I was on fire with the temperature difference. The guys in the Control Tower came running over to see if I was Ok. All I could do was moan "ooooorrrrrrhhhhh!" in some form of pain. They pulled me out of the VP1 and took me to the club house and fed me cherry pie and custard. The worst of it was I had to go back to Redhill and face the cold again!

Enough VP1 for now; just to say she was sold. Being single seat and unable to share these amazing views with anyone, I had to let it go. Twin seat is to share and sharing is more fun. She was brought very cheaply by an intrepid, David Smart and later flown to Spain. Much later it changed hands again. Then years after that it was flipped over on landing and damaged. I don't think it ever was rebuilt. I did make an R/C model of it which featured in RCM&E magazine May2001, the model handled similar to the full size.

Life is stranger than fiction!

Now coincidence can be quite amazing in life but some things are so, so, rare they need to be written up. This has to be one of them and is the key reason why I have written this short ditty of my flying experiences. It all began with G-BKZT a Clutton Fred 1930's style parasol high wing single seat home build aeroplane. She was a shabby red vintage looking plane, run on a shoe string. It was Martins version of the VP1 in that it was his first go, at open cockpit single seat flying. When he got involved with this group I was so pleased that he could now see for himself what I was experiencing

FRED G-BKZT.
VW ENGINE

and he loved it too. I knew he would and we shared tales in the evenings over the telephone.

The only thing that worried me was the way the group serviced and ran the engine side of things. I remember popping over to Fairoaks to see the Fred and felt it looked like the bare minimum in repair was being done. One cylinder was losing compression and it was going to be taken out. I remember thinking if one cylinder is worn the whole engine should be taken out and rebuilt. Martin had more courage than me and flew it a lot. When I flew it I did so with great caution. I flew it like *it* was going to die, at every point. I mean, the propeller going round was a bonus. I flew it like a glider with every field below seen as a stepping stone for a forced landing. I never flew over a town or heavy wooded area. I was not as happy in this, as I was in the now departed VP1 it was fun to fly just not in the best condition mechanically.

My twin brother and I were due to go on holiday in a canal boat on the river Wey departing from Godalming. We were going on holiday with old friends we had known as teenagers. I rang Martin and said to him that I was unable to fly the Fred as I was going on a quick holiday on this canal boat. He said he would fly it and that was that, we thought no more of it.

On the canal boat we went enjoying the river for what it was. My twin loved it most of all and had a passion for boats. One could drink tea eat cake and let him be enthusiastic for you. One night we moored up near an old priory only to hear many fire engines in the distance. These fire engines were one side of the river then they were somewhere else, it was most odd. We asked a couple on the tow path, what was up? They said a red plane had gone down and the fire engines were looking for it. Instantly I thought Martin! Mark said I was crazy; the couple were not sure and if it *was* a plane, it could be any red plane. In any case how often is it 'a plane goes down, the couple must be mistaken?'

Now I had flown the Fred and it was red alright red and dodgy. 'It had to be!'

Mark was having none of it and as the fire engines had gone, 'why bring planes into the conversation yet again.' See this is the way we were. He loved boats I loved planes and we would enthuse and annoy each other over which was best as only two close brothers can.

I had also noticed a light plane circling above and was worried for the fuel tanks draining from one side to the other, which can happen in very prolonged turns. That night I could not sleep thinking about the strange happenings in the sky. We had no further confirmation of a crash and all was silent on the river.

I was told to shut up by Mark in the morning, for fear of spoiling the day. Well I sat on the bow chugging along wondering and worried but silent. We rounded a bend and guess what I saw? The FRED in a field! Yes it was; I did not wait for Mark to moor up but leapt onto the tow path which was a built up embankment. I just made it as the gap was huge. I shouted "Martin!" at the top of my voice. I tripped and slid face down, head first, plunging down to the base of the embankment. My face was covered in stingers and it hurt. Our friends on the boat did laugh to see me do this enthusiastic nose dive.

Martin from his point had flown the Fred the day before and had suffered power loss from the engine. One of the spark plugs had been drilled wrongly, missing the internal web casting in the cylinder head. The plug came out causing the engine to lose power. Martin added more and more throttle to keep flight and plan an emergency landing. Fuel from the faulty cylinder spewed out and ignited. 'The blooming thing caught light,' losing more power all the time. At first he was going back to Fairoaks; then he transmitted he was going to land at a disused strip and then he transmitted "I'm going down!"

There was a fisherman on the canal who was so excited by it all; he came rushing over to Martin as he got out. He said, "it was like world war one! There was all this banging and popping and your plane spluttered down with a plume of smoke pouring from it, swooping in." Martin certainly had a pub story now. He managed to swoop in just missing a fence and got out with a black face the lot. By all accounts it was like some barnstorming film.

The guy I saw circling in the other aeroplane was a mate, who heard the radio transmission and came to relay what was happening to Fairoaks via his radio. Fairoaks airport later called the fire engine search off, with this guys help. Martin camped in the field with the sickly plane sleeping under the wing, for fear of any vandalising of Fred, to keep her safe. The group arrived the following day and were discussing how to de-rig the Fred and get it back to Fairoaks. Martin said "shame we can't pop it on a canal boat and float it out of here, Lloyd is on holiday on the river right now!" As the words left his mouth he was totally spooked by the feint shout that met his ears, which was when I shouted "Martin!" and fell down the embankment.

No I defy anyone to beat that, in the game of chance. It was and still is; to this day such a coincidence. It is such an amazing tale that some people have a job to believe it. Martin and I don't always mention it for fear of losing credibility in a given conversation. Well; we did capture a snippet of VHS film on the day we found Fred in a field, just as we came across it. This was truly amazing.

After meeting up with Martin in the field, the guys all came to the Canal Boat called 'Promise' to drink tea and eat cake. Feeling refreshed and sharing experiences we all helped push Fred out of the field. The day ended but shall never be forgotten.

What have we missed out? Oh! Yes girls.

Those lovely things I had largely avoided. A girl came to our house knowing my twin. She was a stewardess with B.A. She had an Italian mother and British father which gave her black hair and brown eyes. My twin always wanted to do her job on the airlines. He did fly as a steward with another airline in the end, but always wanted to join B.A. as it was the best airline to join. A career of sorts could be had with the right airline as cabin crew with the spinoff of seeing the world, whilst getting paid. I was coerced into the B.A. interview to obtain the interview format and remember questions for my twin brother. This I did, he then went for his interview and failed the second half one to one session. It was such a shame; it was only nerves, as he did make a good steward.

I turned up for the interview; in my, three wheeler and flying jacket and had to use the reception toilets to change into my suit. This made the reception ladies frown a little at me. I later went on to receive a letter saying I had passed. Due to the Gulf war, B.A. put me on hold for a while. They were going to let me know when they wanted me. It was sad for my twin and we nearly changed names so he could fly for B.A. We did not end up doing it as it was illegal but it did cross our minds as we had been muddled up before in our childhood! I was glad I was on hold; as I did not want to spend my life abroad and it saved me writing back to say I did not want the job. Mark, my twin did not see it like that and gave me the hard sell every time we spoke of it. I was working on the railway 'happy as Larry,' only on low pay and working too many hours perhaps.

Now going back to this B.A. girl, she had her own flat and wanted to marry a fine fellow. She was getting to know us when her attention turned slightly on me.

I took her flying and gave her a ride home in my, three wheeler. I urged again and again to put the leather helmet on, but she wanted her pretty hair to flow. When we got back to her flat she was crying with the pain of the cold! Later on another day she telephoned with an invite to a party in Worthing. I accepted with some reservation in my mind as I was not sure of us going out. So we were not alone, I arranged for two younger girls to come as well. I was teaching one of these friends of the family to drive and it would be a good straight run for building confidence. It also would have the effect of keeping it a group exercise.

At the party I met Sarah, a girl with blonde hair blue eyes and a very pleasant look. Her whole countenance impressed me greatly.

She was a giver in life and had no self importance, together with a cheeriness that was easy to be around. She was so lovely in fact; I could not get her out of my mind.

I tried several times to let it go, but this was different. I actually invited her out, in the hope she was *not* quite what I thought and then could be free again. She *was* lovely and therefore needed to be looked after well. I was going to do it as life, in its cruel way, can sometimes crush the really good people. I was not going to let 'some bloke dominate her.' I was going to look after her and give her all she needed to grow and be happy. That was the fourth time we met, yes I had it bad. I was in love for the first time in my life and I could not do anything about it. For someone who just learnt all about aviation control and discipline, this was going to be a little bumpy. I was also from a family of three boys and Sarah was from a family of four girls.

The girl in B.A. at the party gave off a sign, in slight, to Sarah that I was hers. I went to see her at her flat to put things straight. She asked me to put up a picture on the wall and a shelf. She cooked me lunch and later put some nail polish on her toes. I was in the hall and glimpsed her leg exposed in the bedroom. She was an attractive girl but we were not to be and it best I tell her right away, now. It was a little hard and she had a slight tear but as we did not know each other well, it was not too sad. I knew she would soon recover, so I thought of introducing her to a flying chum from South Africa. He was an eligible bachelor and wanted to settle down. This introduction worked and as a courting couple, Sarah and I went to their wedding. My first go at 'match making' and it all worked out amazing.

So off I went, to B.A. as a Long haul Steward.

A while after the Gulf war, a letter came instructing me to have a uniform fit and medical. I had forgotten to write back to B.A. and say I did not want the job after the original interview. My twin brother Mark; being so animated telling me to 'go for it' literally fell off his bed, getting exasperated with my stubborn acceptance of the job offer. You see; I did not want to go *abroad*. My only conception of abroad was when Grant took me to Gozo an island of Malta. We stayed in an apartment that was basic self catering. The apartment was not by the sea as the local man renting had double booked. Things were well let's say basic and only just clean. We had a great time with sightseeing and loved the beaches we found later on. Food also became better when we ate out. So in my small world, I thought my life 'abroad' with B.A. would be very similar. I was also enjoying work, selling tickets on the railway, taking staff up for jolly rides in Chalky's Super Cub on days off.

I was very wrong; as the travel side of things was interesting and enjoyable on the whole. B.A. set up five star Hotels wherever we went and all the transport was arranged running very smoothly. I even stayed in the kings Palace in Jordan, by invitation. The only slight negative was being tired the whole time. The shift and long hours did make crew walk around in a daze most of the time.

The experience of meeting new people understanding cultures and visiting places around the globe was a privilege. I think too it was a life education, in that I did not see a foreign person or place in the same light having visited the country. I did start a count of each country visited but gave up at 65. I never quite fitted in with the stereo typical crew but worked hard for our customers keeping an eye out for the aeroplane and safety of the flight. Having flown as a pilot, the experience was sometimes a useful cohesive link between cabin crew and flight crew.

I opted for a Middle Fleet to increase the variation in destinations around the globe. It was a financially a bad decision paying less money as the flights were medium haul. Long haul; which was the bulk of my career, always had more overtime payments because the flights were longer.

Funny but every time I make a financially unsound decision the story starts again. 'Those who don't know what they are doing for a career, can sometimes lead interesting lives,' I have heard it said. I am beginning to think there is some truth in this.

It was because of this Middle fleet I found myself in Jeddah. Now Jeddah is a country that has no *visitor's visa* and ones passport is left at the airport. This is a little unnerving for the western traveller. After the Gulf war we were not the most popular people as a race and religion plays a part too. In the Middle East Riyadh and Jeddah are religious centres and so one has to show respect for the customs and cultures. There are even religious police. These guys would watch shoppers at the Mall and would whack girl's legs with sticks, whose abiyah was not long enough. They could arrest a girl who pulled the head covering off because of the 30 degree heat! We had a B.A. stewardess attacked in a hotel lift and to keep the diplomatic people happy B.A. asked for male volunteers for these' tricky destinations.' I won't go into it too much but I did volunteer and through boredom in the hotel began to paint oil paintings as these trips were getting regular. *More on this 'artwork' later.*

So for the sake of art I began to photograph Jeddah at night. The trip was only a night stop some 18 hours off and after a sleep one had a short evening and a very early morning start. Instead of another doze, I set off into the night with my trusty camera. It was quite atmospheric looking at an old cedar door or such, a few hundred years old due to the dry heat preserving most wood. The buildings had Moorish architecture and some very interesting styles and shapes, with wooden diamond shaped shutters very different to what we know and see back home. I was going to draw these later or at least show the photos to Sarah.

Now, on the crew brief it stated in bold writing. 'All photography strictly prohibited'.

By way of explanation; the reason I was discreetly snapping away, was really an evolution. I had taken photos at the beach club under water. I had taken shots of the untouched corals in the Red Sea, on a previous visit. Also there was a photographic developing shop opposite the hotel. It did have portraits on display which was a little odd to my mind as I saw no other photo subjects. So my confidence grew. If I was discrete all would be well. After all, my camera was allowed into the country so why could I not take photos?

I photographed inside a Mosque to show Sarah what these places were like. It was also out of my own curiosity that I continued.

Now Jeddah has one of the highest water fountains in the world by an inlet and at night it is lit up with lights. It is actually an up turned oil pump that shoots sea water into the sky. This, I thought, would make a cracking shot. When I arrived; having walked the depth of the city I was delighted it was coloured purple on this night just for me and my camera. What I did not appreciate is; that behind the fountain is the king's palace! Purple lighting of the fountain is to signify his presence in the palace. I took some shots and turned to walk away. An army guard from about 50 yards behind beckoned me over. As I walked away something made me look back. He was more animated now; wanting me to come over and see him. I now calmly walked back over to him. He could not speak English and so I handed him my, 'get out of jail free' card. This was a laminated slip that said we were B.A. crew and our passport was at the airport.

You must understand at this point that crew don't have the same experience in airports as passengers do. Our transition was always swifter and easier with our crew I.D. Also many small diplomatic treats still lingered from the old days that gave some privileges.

For my army guy was on the radio getting me the ok. WRONG! Not on this night, no privileges for being crew this time. A truck appeared I was manhandled into the back; a gun was cocked and pushed into my chest! I had not seen *real guns* up close and hoped the bumps would not set the thing off. Some short ride later and we came to an army compound. It had a parameter wall and a sentry entrance. We went in and I was then escorted in orderly fashion into the main building. It was very plain and military in form. The walls and shapes of the building, being flat and were made from concrete castings. I was passed up the chain of command and I noticed that the personnel spoke better English as we went up the ranks. I ended up with this big General type chap with decoration on his uniform in the form of campaign medals of some sort. Looking at his stature I wondered what they were for, as he did not look athletic in anyway. As I spoke he cut across me and barked, "Have you no respect!" he said pointing to the T.V. It was prayer time and many Muslims on T.V. were walking around Mecca to a prayer. He pushed me into a Sofa and turned the T.V. to face me so that I had a better view. I was in no confusion as to what I was supposed to do.

I had to watch Prayer time and shut up. Arabic Coffee in bent spouted silver jugs was laid out for himself and he spoke to others coming and going from the room. The room was probably the best in the house, so I obeyed in comfort and slight confusion. As I did not understand Arabic I began to think my way out of the situation. My initial fear from the gun ride and such all turned to anger in a subtle way. Odd looking back, but they say this is what can happen, fear turns to anger. They were not going to get my camera, I thought in a cross way. I have a flight in an hour or so and they better tell me what it is they are going to do with me!

This anger soon faded as I thought of the Mosques and 'old Jeddah' that I had photographed. You see, the army guards would not understand about the art in the shots. Would they think of me as some odd kind of spy or reporter?

This country still took people's heads off near the Hotel on a Friday. Stoning was also practiced. One of our crew members stupidly thought he would 'go for a butchers' and see an execution. Needless to say he came back totally traumatised. As he was 'a westerner' the religious police dragged him to the front for a good view. So my anger faded and my head went into clear logic.

I would force the situation and also expose the film. Quietly; with the General sitting opposite, I popped the camera back open. I secretly pulled the film till it was all out. When prayer time had finished I put my camera round my neck, stood up, and leant forward putting the exposed film in his hand. Then; shaking his hand with both my hands, pushing the film into the hand shake, I said. "I'm B.A. crew I didn't realise I couldn't take pictures, sorry." My plan was; I would force the Generals hand, and at least I would know now what was happening. I was running out of time.

I turned and walked out the room turning left down the corridor from whence I'd come. I was expecting him to say something, or call to someone else. I had learnt my lesson and did not turn to look back. I kept up the momentum and soon found myself looking at steps with a sandy yard to the sentry. This open area was an area where it could go wrong so I braved it out, putting on a bold walk to the exit of the compound. I had seen too many films and I imagined bullets dancing round my legs from a guard with shouting. I remember not imagining beyond this, only to walk with boldness like we had to in India some times. I was lucky as there was no noise. The guard lifted the barrier as though he was expecting me, I nodded and walked tall. I wanted to run but waited till about 100 yards then the emotion was too much and I was off. I ran like the wind and did not stop till I reached the Hotel. The city is gridded with two main dual carriageways and it took time to work out the way back, but I ran through the whole puzzle.

Arriving at the hotel I was alarmed to see the crew bus ready to leave. Time had not waited and as I dashed across the reception I saw the other crew members checking out. The crew were saying to each other, 'did you have a nice sleep?' and other pleasantries. I raced up to my room covered in sweat, ran into the shower tearing my clothes off. Cool water calming my nerves but time was ticking. I dressed as best I could and ran down to reception. Thank goodness for clip on ties! I paid cash to the reception and darted on the bus to see the main CSD (cabin services director) frown at my lateness. Being slightly late for the crew bus was a no, no. How would I explain this one?

We had to hand in 12 or so passport slips, in exchange for the passports to be returned at the airport that morning. I was aware that all it would take was one call from the army, to see me heading back to the compound.

I confessed all to Andrea Bennett or 'Sherpa Bennett' a fellow colleague. She was a kind lady with blue eyes and a ready smile who always spoke sense. She loved to travel to the Himalayas and so earned the nick name, Sherpa Bennett. It was a relief to tell someone and get it all out especially that we had not cleared customs yet. She was sympathetic but warned it could go either way with a situation like this. I had broken the law and so could be detained, with the Embassy's wrangling over my release. The airport authorities *didn't* notice one laminated slip missing which was odd as they were so particular about these matters. Off we flew, into the hot morning sun heading for Heathrow again. I was a little wiser and more respectful of these nations' laws after this close call. Phew!

I did have a scary 'pilot error' flight as B.A. crew.

I was new and allowed into the flight deck for landing. I often did this in my career as being a fellow pilot liked to see the professionals at work. The destination was Hong Kong, the old kai Tak airport. It was an interesting approach, as the 747 flew to a hill side navigation aid after which, turning low over houses lined up on finals. At the end of the runway was the sea and it was a tricky airport to land at under normal conditions. This day the weather was terrible. Heavy rain storms with thunder and lightning meant that no airlines were landing. The C.A.A. allow two 'look see approaches' and at about 400ft a decision is made to land or not. On the way in, we were struck by lightning and lost some instrument systems. The 747 is riddled with 'backup systems' and the problem soon rectified itself. But, this sort of thing makes it difficult and busy for the flight crew as you can well imagine.

After our scary two 'look see approaches' we went to the divert airport. The crew were; 'shaken but not stirred.' In a situation like this, the trouble one has is; every other airline is doing the same thing and low on fuel as well. We landed eventually and a little weary I might add. There were no hotel rooms available for crew or passengers and the decision was made to return back to Hong Kong! We were running out of hours. Flight hours or 'crew duty limitation' is a procedure in place for safety. The crew were divided, as some felt we were too tired to carry on and worked out it was too tight on hours. The Captain used his 'discretion' to keep us on duty, making the choice to return. I think our maximum duty was about 19hrs 48mins but don't quote me on this. The new fuel load was wrong; which took time to get right, so we then took off, late. The weather at Hong Kong was still very bad with the rain storms not clearing. No other airline had made a landing as yet, there being six inches of standing water on the runway in parts.

The safer pilot decision would have been to return back to 'the divert' but it would have been filled with shame. Not only would the crew be out of hours but what a waste of fuel the attempt would have been. Therefore the pressure on the Captain to uphold his first decision was immense. We were the first to arrive in Kai Tak and aqua plane down the runway. It was the scariest commercial landing ever, as the flight had two senior crews in disagreement and it was a dangerous atmosphere in the cockpit because of this. How we stopped was 'no one's business' as the standing water did not allow the brakes to work fully, even though set to maximum. We turned off the runway early to avoid the sea, side loading the undercarriage by turning too fast. The 747 400 is a strong aircraft and put up with the abuse. The crew were now 'shaken *and* stirred!'

We put the chocks in at 20:15hrs total flight duty and then spent another five hours stuck in traffic on the crew bus. This was caused by flooding in the tunnel to Honk Kong Island. Most of the crew slept with exhaustion. I was well awake; realising just how a 'wrong decision' can have a compounding effect, even with such a professional outfit as B.A. The chock times were fiddled but later this was found out. The Captain, I heard, lost a stripe over it but this was only hearsay from another crew member.

I can reassure you about Commercial aviation and safety by saying that the industry is great at analysing such things and training better ways of operation after every incident. The flying as a whole in my career was 90% safe but I would also say it became better and better from a safety point of view, even in my 15 years of service.

On a lighter note going back to the art; a trip in Botswana was funny.

I was painting oil painting with quick drying gel to add value to the time down route. One could not always sightsee and 'pleasure hunt' the whole time, as the costs involved were using money which paid bills back home. I was not a heavy drinker or party goer and did not sit around the pool sunbathing. Having said all this, on this day I did visit the pool area to see the crew. I was painting a portrait from a

'Hello' magazine on a canvas board A4 in size. This was a way of passing time and going home feeling it was not wasted time.

The painting was not drying quickly enough, so I put it on my balcony in the sunshine. I went off on a 'walk about' seeing what I could see. When I arrived back to the Hotel the African door keeper had blue oil paint on his hands. I was lucky to spot it and made an enquiry at the reception. The reception staff too had bright oil paint on their black skin. I was so embarrassed when they gave me back the picture, which had also collected some grass. I apologised profusely and went to my room to fix the damaged image again.

Many hours later I was really pleased with the image and went to see the crew at the pool. The crew had been suffering the comments of a senior first officer who was too flirty with the girls. He was also quite arrogant and had been a 'bit of a bore' to be around. I had not known this situation as I had been out in the morning walking. I showed the picture to the sunbathing girls and then placed it on a table to absorb more of the sun's rays, hoping it would now dry. The first officer was wearing dark navy blue shorts and came over to talk to the girls again, much to their grief.

He sat on my picture thinking it was just a 'Hello' magazine or such. After all, he had probably flicked through one mid flight at some point, as it was a magazine we carried on board the aircraft at the time. I gasped! But then did not quite have the courage to say anything, as he was not too approachable. As he was rebuffed with his advances to the girls; he swaggered off with the perfect imprint of my painting on his short bottoms! No one said a word. But when he had gone the laughter began. It did not stop in Botswana, as at the following destination Harare, the first officer attended the pool again, this time with long trousers on. I was very keen to keep the finished product from his view on the two return sectors back to Heathrow, not easy.

Our courtship had a lovely flying tale to go with it and some great moments to share.

When abroad I was never completely 'tip top' as my heart was always at home in the sense that I missed Sarah. This feeling stayed with me throughout my career and contributed to me leaving B.A. later on. Somewhere around this time Sarah and I started a year of courtship that had some turbulence to report about. We always loved each other, but put our families first and this caused some bumps for us. Although I was 27 and had some real life experience with work and flying I had a lot to learn with matters of love and family.

Moving now in time to the 5th April 1995 and I was to fly the Fred for one last time. One small coincidence was; that I found out a group member of the Fred who was the main engineer from Rushett Farm all those years ago, now worked for B.A. I was not a group member and had the odd fly by invitation only. I had a few flights in Fred, this story being the last flight in her. Incidentally FRED is an acronym for; **F**old able **R**oad able **E**conomical **D**esign.

Sarah was on holiday with her family atCamber Sands Pontins on the edge of East Sussex. This was a five day stay and I was at a loose end, so elected to fly the Fred which was now at based Whitewaltham. I worked out with the North West wind I could fly to Headcorn a good place to spend an afternoon. The fuel range of the Fred was not good with about two hour's maximum fuel at some 60kts or so of speed. With this tail wind I could get there in one hit. So it was that I took off in this little red aeroplane travelling east. What was strange is the forecasts we used to get for flying were very accurate and it was often that we calculated the wind drift to exact fuel use. It was spot on most of the time but something odd happened this day.

As I climbed today, the upper wind was a lot quicker. I made a quick calculation as the aircraft chugged along and realised I could go further. This was strange because my mind must have been on Sarah and her stay, for I decided to fly to Lydd in Kent. This airport was not in my log book and that was good enough for me. Sitting there at a reasonable height; enjoying the view and spring air I thought I might climb as high as I could, given the airspace restrictions and see what else the wind would reap. Well, it reaped more in my favour and I soon hatched a plan to glide down over Camber Sands on finals for Lydd. I would take a snap, with my Olympus camera and at least I would have something to talk about the next time we met. I could say, 'Was this where you stayed?' showing the snap, just for a bit of fun.

Sarah for her part was walking with her family to her car; they were looking to drive out for the day from Camber Sands Holiday Park. She looked up and noticed a red aeroplane. Now Sarah is no plane spotter and she was going on a feeling. Her father wanted to go out with the car but her mother was in tune with her feelings more and let her go. Yes Sarah grabbed the keys from her dad and put her little sister in the car and took off towards the way the aeroplane went. This was a bold move and out of character for Sarah at the time. It was a gamble as she did not know the local area but Sarah wanted to be with me too, deep down.

To add depth to the story our families had fallen out and there were disagreements all around. Together alone we were calm and good for each other. My mother in law could see this but my father in law thought otherwise. We were getting to know one another and only I was sure very early on. Sarah had a young German chap interested in her at the very start and was awaiting his reply which turned out to be on and off. These things all foxed Sarah who was making up her own mind up. The family issues served to get her head in a spin and to make it hard going for both of us.

At this point I felt I was scaling a big wall and was running out of energy fast. Some of it was the distance we lived apart; some of it was my crazy shift work, piling on a new kind of fatigue. All things were seemingly set against us and this day was defiantly a crucial moment in time. To describe the fatigue; I remember taking a guy flying and having arrived back from Japan the day before I was tired but thought I was fine to fly. At Redhill aerodrome I could hear what the tower was saying but was unable to respond properly. I was in a strange mist of tiredness. I realised I was operating unsafe because of crew fatigue. I cancelled the flight on the taxi way and went home disappointing my passenger. It was a strange thing working our bizarre rosters, flying from Japan to Los Angeles to India to.....This with the family issues and travel added up. In short our courtship was hard and I was in need of reassurance.

So I took the snap of Camber Sands holiday camp leaning out the cockpit and set Fred into the landing circuit with about 12 minutes of fuel left. It felt a long way in the cramped cockpit and it was hard to sit it out for the duration. Lydd seemed huge and I flew along the wide runway to the taxi exit, to flare right near the exit, all in a cross wind. It was working a treat this flight and a good choice of destination. I asked about fuel at the apron area and soon found myself topping up. Fred was brimmed full as I had a heavy wind to battle, on the way back. I was signing in the visiting log when I looked up and there was Sarah! I said "Hi!" automatically and looked down but then the penny dropped. It was Sarah and it was amazing to see her right now, right here!

How did she get here? How did she know I was here, and what about the timing of it all? We had many questions to be answered from each other and a strange feeling of 'it was meant to be.' We sat and had coffee and chatted, we needed to talk and be alone from our parents. We had no family pressure that day and we could both see we mattered to each other. We hugged a long hug we both needed the reassurance of affection which ended our worries. I was feeling so much better and this hug topped me up to carry on with the courtship.

I remember asking for an early right turn and departed low right over the main building and waved down at Sarah and her sister in the car park. On the way home I flew as low as I could to avoid the wind that had guided me to Lydd. It was late evening when I arrived at Whitewaltham and the little red plane looked small and sorry as I left it in the large hanger. I somehow sensed that I would not fly her again. I wished Fred was better loved but thought no more of it as I had a different love to attend to right now.

I flew abroad in some light aircraft when down route, with the airline.

I flew from Charles Prince Airport with its 1200 meter long runway; in a little yellow Piper cub but the J3, or underpowered version. We were hot and high, both these factors affecting the performance. The heat gives the wings less air molecules to work with and the prop gives less thrust too. The high air is less dense due to atmospheric pressure being lower. So hot and high is a double negative with flying. We used so much runway in Z-MFC it was astounding! I had flown Super Cubs and even an old L13 all from the same breed, but this was another ball game. I had to hold it in ground effect for what seemed a life time on takeoff, just to get the other side of the drag curve! We staggered into the air with the stall so close all the way. This was especially noticeable in some heat turbulence. We, my local guide and I, went north east to a game reserve and watched the animals below. These views were very memorable and so different to flying back home.

The only down side to flying in Africa is maintenance and worn parts being unavailable. On an aircraft bolt it has a tiny x mark on the head. This is a symbol that lets you know it has an approximate 7:1 ratio, for tensile force. In other words it will break at 7 tons to hold 1 ton in normal use. Sometimes in desperation or ignorance car bolts can be found on these tired old aeroplanes. I only flew once in central Africa.

Another short sortie came again in the USA.

Now I must say the USA is very trusting in many ways. I went on a casual jaunt to Oakland Sanfrancisco. I was going to fly from Hayward but there was a conversation pointing to more interesting aircraft being flown at Oakland Municipal. I did not want to fly in a' spam can' on a hot day. Call me fussy; but when you have flown open cockpit, it becomes the only way. Off I went on my quest and walked to the other side near runway 27. As you well know the folks over the pond don't walk if they can drive. Most of this is the sheer size of areas used to build on. So it was not easy in the summer heat with no paths, but I was determined to have a flying day of sorts. I started chatting to some guy's, operating two PT17 Boeing Stearman biplanes. They were banner towing with these old wartime trainers. One of these was white and had a supercharger on the engine. The other Stearman was painted in WW2 blue and yellow trainer colours. My first impression was the noise of the aircraft and I was intrigued about the different way they get the banners hooked up.

In England banner towing is not common and I only once saw, an S shape rope laid out in such a way to take up the snatch of the initial aircraft pull. It was attached to the aircraft pre flight. This was observed at Headcorn and it was too far to see the operation in detail.

The aircraft here in the USA; had a small rope attached to the tail area with a 'dirty great hook' on the end of it. The difference was, the pilot would take off, throw this short rope down and out of the cockpit being careful not to hit his tail with it. He would then fly a low pass where the hook would catch a lasso rope from the banner. The banner was laid out flat and the lasso rope held up about 5 ft, with plastic poles and cones to mark out this pick up point.

The pilot would have to go in at full charge to pick up the Banner. The banner would drag all the airspeed away in an instant, when taking to the air behind the aeroplane. The aeroplane would climb away with two huge Bacardi adverts or such at full chat. This was the way it was done state side. This day the banner was laid out to the south side of an active runway.

I soon started to chat to the father and son who ran it all and watched with interest. I spoke of my limited flying experience and they seemed *very* interested in what I had flown. After a few hours the father came over and asked if I wanted a go. This always amazes me how trusting and hospitable our folks over the pond are. I mean; I had never banner towed or flown a Stearman biplane before, but they were very trusting to let me try.

As I sat in the PT17 Boeing Stearman, I certainly felt I was in an American made, hunk of aeroplane.

The cockpit was bigger than a Stampe or Tiger Moth and the engine seemed huge. I was amazed at the size of the exhaust pipe pointing at me both sides. Now these babies have no silencer and when she was fired up, it was deafening. This was a lasting memory. It was heavy; deafening, full of drag, but did have steady easy handling. That is how I would describe a Stearman, from my short flight. You feel safe; only an engine out, would be landing directly below. Don't plan a glide ahead if the engine fails; look to land below should it happen. It felt very strong with its heavy duty, well, everything.

With deafening noise I took off and climbed out, it was so nice not to be trolling round shops or wasting time downtown. I flew an orbit and threw the hook down and out. Then I looked forward to diving low across the active, towards the pickup plastic poles. They were hard to see but I crossed them square on with full power set; I waited, but no pick up. I thought, 'Blimey I have to come in lower!' This I did, there was no means of communication with the ground and I felt they would watch me and shake their heads if I had it all wrong. A ground handling lady who was part of the banner company; watched me but I had no signal. The next dive I came in, mega low. I was not used to being flat out inches up and held my breath to get it right. Elevator sensitivity does increase and you can over pitch a little, not good; feet above the ground. I went in so low the wing dinked one on the white plastic poles and I still did not pick it up the banner! I sussed the point that I was too low, on both times and set to put it right on the next pass. This was becoming embarrassing.

Next go, perfect and the hook up of the banner decimated my airspeed. It felt as though I had decelerated into a big pillow, or flown into some invisible Marsh Mellow. The airspeed indicator unwound and I staggered away. The rest of the flight was like flying an aircraft with a sickly engine, such was the drag from the banner. I went over the bay area which seemed dodgy, as Sanfrancisco bay is no place for an engine out. I flew along the Piers of Downtown and back to Oakland to jettison the banner away. It was odd to watch it fall and I was pleased with my target dropping. It was good to get some vital speed back. I did not abuse the time given to me and landed right away. On landing the torque from the huge Propeller caught me out a tad, in yawing me as I shut the throttle, wheeling the brute on. This was slight, but a reminder that I did not know this American beast.

When I taxied back and shut down, a ground crew Lady in the blue base ball cap, pointed out I was too low at first and that I had bent the hook. What I had done in flying low was, bounce the hook on the active runway which then skipped high into the air over the lasso. The plastic pole being touched was not mentioned and they were then busy packing up for the day. I offered to pay for my flight but they said no and offered me beer and a lift. This I refused as they had given this stranger enough. I walked home and back to the 'Bart train' system to get me 'downtown' as they say. How would I tell the crew about this one? Sometimes my life seemed bizarre and perhaps only the flight crew should know as they would be more likely to understand.

A lesson had in 'listening to ones wife.'

On the motor bike noise was a big issue on communication. The 110 bhp performance engine and wind all play their parts to make communication difficult. As we only had a motorcycle at the time Sarah did ride pillion a few times but it was rare for safety reasons. I always found the bike handled worse and stopping distance increased. I think Sarah rode about three times in total. Our wedding was a rushed affair because of difficulties with family wishes. Not going in too much detail as this could be another story, my family did not attend in protest, which was a shame. We had a sit down meal in a bowling club house with 40 people in attendance. Someone kindly put a model passenger Jet on the cake; to connect with all the flying, but it had my twin brother's airline livery on it which made me cry. I did so want him to come at least Mark for some 'twins reason.'

Still in my mind the point of getting married is to seal a lifelong bond and what happens after, is far more important than detail of the big day. It had enjoyable moments in it and it 'did the job' as they say. Previous to this wedding with family arguments brewing, I went to the cash till drew £800 gave it to Sarah and said I'm off to China when I get back we'll get married. She arranged it in 10 days flat with the help of friends and her family. This way by Sarah and I paying and arranging it would be *our day* and easier to control for harmony. We also realised together we were strong and it was outside issues wearing us down.

Looking back now if we had been more focused about *our* needs as a couple and less family pleasing, or outward looking, we would have fared better early on. At the time though, you go with the experience you have and are who you are, then. Any regrets one has in life can soon become unsolved questions, as each person grows with time. The early moves we make cannot be projected forward into our decisions now. We learn what really matters, sometimes *after* it is needed.

I came off the flight the next day, paid the gas bill in the town Post Office and was married by two pm. My father in law gave Sarah away and performed the ceremonial speech. This speech was about Alcock & Browns' non- stop transatlantic flight 1919 taking off and crash landing in a bog in Ireland *but,* making it to the other side. It was very apt and made the friends and family in attendance laugh all 100 or so.

My full size flying was coming to its autumn years.

I hired a Chipmunk for aerobatic training from Shoreham and had a 10th share of an awful Luton Minor. It was a great group but a dreadful aeroplane. I only flew it twice as it was a heap. All the members bar two were so scared of it, they would not fly her. This made the airborne costs very cheap for the two of us who were brave enough to give it a go. Later the group invested in Building Society shares and the shares paid out changing things. Suddenly we had thousands of pounds and the group brought a nearly new pylon racer which was to be my last ever share. But first, we must talk of the Luton Minor flight from Shoreham.

G-BBCY was a silver doped green striped parasol aeroplane like the Fred, but bigger and so seemingly offering more. Physically getting into it was a nightmare. You had to lean right over the cockpit and look over the other side, whilst somehow putting in a leg. Then you had to ease in the other leg. Next you would wriggle to get seated down in. Getting out was easier. I just pulled myself out with the jury struts, arriving unceremoniously head first on the floor. The under carriage was not like the VP1, it was spindly with a bicycle brake leaver set up. This was so ineffective in stopping it took time and lots of desperate squeezing. The engine was another example of a group neglecting maintenance; it was tired and a sorrowful thing to look at.

It was a cool day on my first flight; but there was some thermal activity, as the sun was out and warming the land up. I was going to Whitewaltham to meet Martin on the off chance and took off heading east. Now I was half way down the runway which surprised me a little because these home builds were usually off earlier. Ahead lay the river and rising ground with the bungalows of Shoreham town. To the right was sea and my plan was to turn left or north. On the north heading was the M27 with its road bridge across the river. The air around the airfield was buoyant and full of lift. This gave me a false reading of this aircrafts performance.

As I passed the parameter I began to sink slightly with full power over the river. I was established in my turn north and looked at the road. I started thinking of an early left turn inside the airfield perimeter and precautionary landing, it was that tight. She raised enough to stagger over the road bridge and I continued north. As I was tracking the river, I was in more sink. This sink was equal to the Luton's climb but, it did inch up. I now had the College to my left and Truleigh hill to my right. Both were high ground. I was aware not to keep her on the back of the drag curve and pinned the climb speed. Next obstacle was some power lines. 'Do I stall over the top and risk it, or do I fly under them?' I thought. Well this was a first; I flew *under them* for safety sake.

It took me till Dunsfold to get 1500ft. I started flying it like a glider in the end and it did improve in the climb. Back on the ground at Whitewaltham I fell out of her in the way I had worked out previous. I stood up and went straight round to the engine, to see if there was any sign of failure. Guess who strolled over? He was watching me scratching my head peering at the engine. John Timms! "How the devil are you? Long time no see." Etc. He was a great engineer and pulled the prop through several times. "It has low compression on number two. These are so underpowered that you need them tip top, but the lack of power is cylinder number two." He said this with discernment the way only he could. "You don't own a share in this heap, do you?" I told him I did, sheepishly and he laughed. We went off and had tea. I can't remember Martin showing or not on that day but I remember the takeoff. My plan was to go back home and insist to the group that the engine be hauled out and rebuilt.

I took off having noticed a ploughed field to the left. My plan was to circle it until it gave a thermal to me. A tractor was ploughing in earnest and he must have wondered why I was circling over him so low. I bet it looked odd from the airfield side too. Soggy old Luton Minor, drops below the tree line to a ploughed field and circles low. I kept my turns shallow and concentrated hard on speed. Eventually, I caught a good thermal and was off. It took me high and set me up for the way home.

On the journey home I started to think that flying junk was a little dangerous and this was wearing thin. If the group rebuilt the engine fine if not I was out of it. You see being married now I wanted money for the house too and had someone to look after. The money I spent flying had felt like *our* money and so spending heavily on flying for fun was not fair to Sarah. I was considering hanging up my goggles. Lady luck shone on me, as the group sold the Luton minor to the only other inside group member, who was brave enough or silly enough to fly it. The Building Society's shares paid out and I inherited a shiny new hot pylon racer. 'Jammy or what!'

Sadly the Luton taxied out of Shoreham again soon after and a young chap called Malcolm was on short finals in his new Jodel D9. He swerved in the flare to miss the Luton Minor, crashed into a caravan and died. The guy in the Luton was unaware of his involvement having not seen the D9 on finals. Martin knew Malcolm well and it was all very sad. Flying full size aircraft bites down hard, in real life and this sort of thing was always very sobering.

I flew our group's new aircraft once and it was a very hot ship. So hot, that I felt I should fly it often to 'keep current on it.' She had a high landing speed and was short coupled. One had to be fast, early accurate with the controls, on takeoff and in the landing flare. It was like a mono plane 'Pitts Special' in shape. I later made the final decision that to fly my new mount more; was not fair to Sarah, financially. To fly it less, would be deadly due its demanding handling. So that was the last of my full size flying. I sold the share; we brought furniture, or some other house nesting purchases and that was that.

Some of the money was used to purchase a vintage style JZR three wheeler, to keep the wind in the hair as I knew flying was winding down.

Remember the Lomax 223 front wheel drive three wheeler. Well JZR was a rear wheel drive three wheeler and handled very differently. It was a British racing green colour and more akin to the Morgan three wheeler of 1930's fame. The front suspension had to be set up correctly. I had my tools out in the road to do this on my new purchase. It had just been built and needed understanding and checking. It was my first proper day off I had had from work. My mother in law came round to see me. I thought people were more important than jobs and we went for a ride; with my past three wheel car experience working against me. I noticed a tail of traffic behind me as we were in no hurry enjoying the cold but sunny day. I came out of a roundabout into a notoriously sharp bend which tightened up. I had been all around the local roads but never experienced this bend. It came in hard with the wrong camber tightening up. The body of the car articulated in the soft suspension set up. The back end sat down on the exhaust and body work. This caused the tail to come round and 'over steer' in an instant. I rolled the open top vintage three wheel car.

The accident was very graphic. I came round from a bump to the head and wriggled out from under the upside down car. I tried to lift the car from my mother in law and managed to get it on its side. It is amazing the strength one has when adrenaline is running high. A bystander had a penknife and helped me cut her free from the entangled seat belt. It was very hard seeing a person I loved broken. She had split her face on a bollard and I could see her skull. Her lung was punctured and this I knew because the blood in her mouth was bright in colour. I managed to put her in a recovery position and shouted to the people looking on, to call for an ambulance but they were too shocked at seeing the mess to respond properly. I remember eventually screaming at them to telephone and then passed out. As I came round a helicopter arrived and took her away and I went in for observation at the local hospital. Oddly my injuries were light, only because I did not have my seat belt on.

This accident shattered the worlds we had lived in and affected everyone in my wife's family.

My mother in law, ended up in hospital for a year with a broken back being resuscitated three times and more. The injuries lasted to see her wheelchair bound for life.

My father in laws life changed beyond recognition and needless to say he was not pleased with his new son in law. Sarah and I had our own emotions to deal with and those which were raw around us. Relationships with both families were at this time very, very strained. It was a dark time with hardly any days of joy to be had.

This time and circumstance again could fill a book, but is mentioned in brief to give insight into how things changed. One thing I had to do; a few months after the accident, was get into a Chipmunk and go through some aerobatic flying drills. My confidence as a person was in tatters and I needed to see if I was shot completely. I flew very well and was surprised as I expected worse from my piloting. When I landed, I knew I was still me, deep inside and could perhaps one day recover. The flying helped me that day, it was a bridge to connect back to the world that was, in some way. I think some things that are really bad, one learns to live with, rather than get over in life. I still had a few adventures in aircraft to come and each one a warm memory.

A testimony to my father and mother in law is that we all get along now; such is the power of forgiveness and love in the family. We always loved each other and sought out the others interest, but this accident was a massive challenge to all the family. It has taken many years of effort but we have achieved what most could not.

Motorcycling featured as a way of overcoming boredom getting to work.

The trundle to Heathrow was tedious and tense as traffic jams could make you miss your trip. As crew your roster would be wiped clean if this happened. You could not plan home life and you went off on all the low paid trips, till the roster was built up again. It could cost over £500 in wages lost for one late trip and was very inconvenient back home. Basically you were never late even if it meant turning up to work an hour and a half before each flight.

After the accident I did not like driving, also having a passenger next to me felt too much. I then walked past a shop in Worthing called 'Alf's Motorcycles.' Seeing these machines all lined up outside gave me an idea, to beat the traffic to work and release me from driving cars. Off I went, to Brighton CSM School of motorcycling and came back with my motorcycle licence five days later. It was a great course and I was pleased to pay extra to learn more for safety sake. I had several motorcycles and one or two stories particularly when biking up from Cornwall to Heathrow which happened later.

One modelling *and* motorcycling story of note begins with a model Spitfire from Mick Reeves model shop. This was a balsa Spitfire some 60 inch wing span and a built up block shaped front nose. I hated going to Hotels and wasting valuable time. Time at home always seemed rushed and after D.I.Y. and visiting friends I seemed to be off to work again. I was getting back into teaching model flying and had a keen student Mathew Ivey. He was a large tall blonde haired window cleaner. I called him 'Cheesy' because when we went flying he was always smiling. I did rent the 'Chippy' one more time to give him a flight in the real thing but full size flying was winding right down. Anyway I wanted to build the Spitfire abroad and fly it back at home.

Now the box was huge and certain things we were not allowed to carry on board the B.A. aircraft modelling knives being one of them. So I had to use all my imagination and whit to have a way of constructing whilst in the Hotel. I took for example, the handle of the knife and purchased the blades down route. The way I managed to get round the extra large model box on a Motorcycle was; to get dressed in my leathers and have Sarah sellotape the huge box to my back with me holding my arms up. The tensile strength of sellotape is strong in pull. Now, the motorcycle was a Laverda 668 sports bike and being Italian it was relatively small. With me sitting down, the box was slightly larger than my head and wider than my body. This wider box created some drag and limited my speed on the motorway to 55mph, beyond that the sellotape began to stretch alarmingly. People on the motorway when passing me looked with puzzlement at who was behind the box.

I thought I was clever to have made it safely all the way and produced my scissors to cut myself free from the box in the B.A. car park. It had all worked, "yes!" The B.A. crew building was a purpose made building on the Bath Road which had a clever airside area where the crew were sealed into the bus which would drive straight to the aircraft. We had a system with crew baggage and items you wished to take abroad, being x-rayed first. I managed to get the 'big box' with me on the flight. What was funny was a senior crew member said in the briefing that she saw the oddest thing on the motorway. She saw 'a large cardboard box riding a motorcycle!' I kept quiet not wanting to lose credibility too early. I then had to avoid her in the crew baggage area……not easy with a big box!

So at the Hotel room I was so pleased to be able to build and make my time productive. Trouble soon lured as the rooms were very posh. I glued the parts over the box but soon found sanding balsa wood a problem. I called to reception for a vacuum cleaner. Trouble again, because the hotel cleaner wanted to vacuum up *for* me. This was not fair to her and embarrassed me. So I hit on a plan, to sand outside on my balcony. I had a lot of sanding as I had no razor plane, because of the security measures. The nose and fuselage in the main; of this kit, is block balsa and took some sanding. I started with very course grit to remove material and became lost in the moment, sanding in the Californian sun on my balcony. As I finished with fine grit, I blew the last dust away to marvel at the way the Spitfire could now be seen through what was lumpy blocks. What lovely lines a Spitfire has, I thought. Magic!

I then looked around and saw our female crew in their bikinis below, about three floors down sun creamed up. They had shades on, head phones on, and were sleep like in posture. They were oblivious right now to the white balsa dust that covered them! The wind had been just right to blow it right on them. I had dusted them with my Balsa dust and it seemed to stick with the cream. Gulp! What had I done! I quietly slid the balcony glass door shut and proceeded to do all sanding in the shower. This worked well as I could use the shower head to clean up the dust. I finished the Spitfire and at 'check out time,' the crew thought I had purchased the Spitfire readymade in L.A. I made little of it. I did however; catch the tail end of a conversation with the girls about 'Hotel building work causing problems at the pool, which was hotly denied by the Hotel staff.'

For the journey home I bound the front fuselage to the motorcycle seat with my trusty sellotape and bound the wing on too. The wing now being 60 inches long and the passenger seat a mere pad, it did look rather odd with all this over hang. I had a new problem on the ride home. As I reached 40mph the tail of the Spitfire fluttered posing serious risk of damage to the model. I had been through so much with this build I did not want to damage it further. So 35-40mph was my top speed round the M25 and A3 needless to say, many people looked at me. It was a painful slow ride home that day but worth it in the end.

I went on to build three model aircraft in a similar way, just for the heck of it. A Flair Harvard, (Picture RCM&E Jan 2001 pg.54) also a Flair Black Magic the later being built in two days flat. This 'build off' was from kit to finished model, covering, radio, the lot! It was a marathon and sprint build, quite exhausting but well worth it as it was a great little flyer. I did however *show* the box to the crew at the briefing on the next two builds. This eased my tensions in the baggage area and kept the embarrassment levels manageable. I also looked at the box size before purchase. The kit boxes incidentally; were later adapted to help with the transit back home.

A Shiny new red sports bike 'dinked!'

I prided myself on wearing the proper clothing when motorcycling. I reasoned that *if* I did have a 'spill,' at least I had done all I could to protect myself. I purchased a second hand leather race suit for £700 which had red flames on the back. It was not my choice only the one that fitted my tall body. It was rather; well let's just say garish and racy. I had just purchased a new red sports bike which had, 'a go faster head in the clocks riding position.'

This day Sarah needed some milk for cooking, quick, and the bike was outside having just been cleaned. I dressed in a hurry but put on some Timberland lace up boots as opposed to my normal bike boots. Our local shopping parade had a pedestrian crossing right in the centre, which was always very busy with pedestrians and traffic alike. I filtered to the front of the traffic queue right up to the crossing. I watched an old lady cross the road complete with her 'tartan coloured' wheelie basket with white spoke wheels. As I stopped I could not put my leg down. The Timberland boot laces had entangled in the bike. I was in a sitting position on my racy red sports bike as the world turned 90 degrees on its side! The worst of it was, the old lady rushed over to help me back up again. Imagine me in my flame covered race suit and on a shiny new red sports bike, getting assistance from the 'old dear.' Thank goodness for the helmet covering my complementary red face! I dinked the mirror.

Going back in time a tad; our Honeymoon was, Sarah coming on my next trip as a married partner but me working the flight.

Now I had done several flights with the same check in time and felt I knew the time off by heart. Sarah and I the next day were heading up to Heathrow on the motorcycle. Sarah had to pack all she needed in one backpack with my clothes. This was hard for her being a woman and us sharing a small bag. It was a two sector trip over four days giving, a clear day and a half for sightseeing. All went to plan but we were close on time. The weather was fine for October.

At Heathrow I dropped off Sarah at terminal four and went to the crew building Compass centre. As I swiped my I.D. to 'check in,' a red screen alerted me I had missed the flight! This was due to America daylight saving time changing the departure time. Sarah had checked in and was on the aircraft bound for San Francisco, she had no money with her as I had it. I went to the crew desk and the operations staff said they had put me on the Narita flight to Japan!

From Sarah's' point of view she boarded the flight asked for my whereabouts and was told I had not made the flight and the crew were waiting for a standby crew member.

At this point I must say B.A. does not hold an aircraft, for any 'one passenger' or crew member and standby duties cover such events.

I pleaded with the desk telling them the story of Sarah and our little honeymoon. I was lucky as I was sent to the ramp area in a Transit van, with the instruction that if the standby crew arrived first they would go. I made it just in the nick of time! Sarah was at the door of the aircraft. It was on an outside ramp area with steps up to it. The engines were running. My van driver had beaten the standby crew to the aircraft and we went very flustered but, heading off to San Francisco. Phew!

On the flight, the crew kept Sarah's wine glass topped up being told some of the stories of our bumpy courtship. Now Sarah was no drinker, in fact quite the opposite and she was topped up well by our crew. Later we were given some Champagne and I was keen to try it after a stressful trip. Which we did; that night and being a bottle of Krug it went down very well indeed. Next morning Sarah did not feel too well, which was such a shame and a disappointment for us both. I was really concerned and worried about food poisoning or such. She recovered by lunch time only that; over the bay in Sausalito, I ordered another bottle of wine for us to try. She enjoyed the sights but felt a tad queasy and rough. In our naivety it was the wine that was making her feel 'off colour.' We actually worked this out six months later. Such was our slow development in 'worldly' matters up till now. You could say we were both a little old fashioned, in upbringing I mean.

A little while later, we went on a proper holiday to a tropical island and relaxed, so we did get a proper honeymoon holiday in the end.

As Sarah had missed out a little in Frisco I went back with her using the motorcycle again.

Our communication on the bike was; a tap on the leg meant yes. Now my Sarah is a talker and on the way up to Heathrow she was talking. With the noise of the bike I could not understand what she was saying, so tapped her occasionally on the leg. 'Yes, Yes, Yes!' This happened all the way to a fuel station in Leatherhead. My focus was on the flight time as I did not want a repeat in, nearly missing the flight. WRONG! *You must listen to your wife.*

"I'm glad you have my passport" she said at the petrol pumps. "What! I don't have it!" I said in astonishment. "Why did you say yes, I asked you several times" she said annoyed. Sarah was right I had not listened! Time now was really against me again. I had to think fast, I dropped Sarah at friends who could drive her back home.

These friends lived in Godalming and incidentally were the same friends as were on the Canal boat years ago when we found Martin in the field.

I had to ride extremely fast up the A3 towards Heathrow to catch the flight. I was sad to leave Sarah and was beginning to feel Frisco was jinxed in some way. When I arrived in my Hotel room 'state side,' I flopped on the bed and the phone rang. It was Sarah she had gone back home and was catching the flight the next day!

What it meant for me was sleeping, getting up and collecting Sarah at the airport the next day. We would have 18hrs sightseeing! We did it and did enjoy it all, steering clear of too much wine we had a great time. We were both tired as we packed it all in. I had been many times before and knew just what to see and how.

The Captain was a great guy and looked at Sarah saying: "My dear; you do look tired, I'll pop you in 'First' so you can sleep." This was a privilege and one Sarah enjoyed. I cooked up her breakfast on board in the morning which was nice to do as I had often missed Sarah at work. The First officer's mother was a little posh and was sitting in 'First' next to Sarah. On the arrival to Heathrow she said to Sarah "Dear; have you transport to take you home?" She was looking at the sheet rain outside on the tarmac. Sarah had not the heart to tell her she would be on the M25; in heavy traffic, with the rain soaking her on Lloyd's motorcycle! She could never have airs and graces.

Sarah was soon working in a local cottage Hospital in Arundel.

She needed reliable transport so I purchased a new Suzuki Vitara. This car cost slightly more than anticipated and left me with no money whatsoever. My crew Diners Card, for drawing out allowances down route, would allow £250 cash withdrawal. 'What could I get that was reliable transport me to Heathrow?' The answer came from India and Japan. Half the population of India travel on Honda step through mopeds. Whole families would travel miles on the humble C90 and I mean whole families clinging on! Honda built its vast company on these humble mopeds sold abroad. For £250 I could get a second hand one. If it was good enough for a family in India, it was good enough for me I reasoned.

This was fine to a point the top speed was a stumbling block. The A3 and M25 were not to forgiving roads to any vehicle travelling at 50mph. I therefore put my head in the clocks and stretched the throttle cable, to achieve a 55mph max. I would lie flat to reduce the wind drag resting my feet on the passenger foot pegs. This high speed action wore the engine out in no time at all. We used to work a back to back flight in B.A. which was a four sector trip. This would be Heathrow to New York, New York to Heathrow, Heathrow to Chicago and back to Heathrow. We would get say 12 hours off in Heathrow to rest between sectors. I would always go home as even six hours in my own bed was better for me emotionally than to stay away from home yet again. I would always miss Sarah and six days away, was getting too long.

So this rush hour morning the old C90 step through moped 'let go' and the engine seized. It stopped with full morning traffic flow on the M25. I was in the drizzle, right where the hard shoulder had been removed to make another carriageway. Sound protective fencing and barriers were to my left side and large lorries threatening to drag me under them, to my right. I was 'stuck between a rock and a hard place.'

I got off the bike and that made my width even wider. I could now see how unfortunate people are sometimes dragged under Lorries when there was no hard shoulder as a refuge. To reduce my width, I sat back on the bike and shushed it along with my legs, like a toddler who is sitting on their first wheeled toy. This moped had no pedals see. This action got me to the nearest point where I could safely get off it. I tried to pull the moped over the barrier, but it seemed a dead weight. I managed to wheel it up on the barrier to manhandle it to an open swinging gate. This was part of the sound proof fencing at the side of the motorway. The moped was a dead weight, so I pushed it off the barrier through the open door. There was a steep embankment the other side and it, up ended, to fall front over back several times. Crash! It went right down to the bottom. I knew at this point it was wrecked. If the motor *was* repairable, now I had 'totalled it!'

I slid down the wet embankment to be confronted with a nine foot exclusion fence and barbed wire. I scaled this to pop out in the garden of a bungalow in suburban Byfleet. It must have looked odd me appearing in someone's garden unannounced. I tried to make nothing of it, even though a neighbour looked twice at me. My mind was on getting home and as fast as possible as I now had things to sort out. I thought 'Byfleet, great, a train ride home.' walking for the station.

So that was how I travelled all the way back home. Changing trains from Byfleet, Clapham, Gatwick and then Gatwick to Arundel. I then had a four mile walk or so to Burpham. I arrived late evening to find Sarah had gone to work and I had no front door keys. She was working the night shift and I had left the keys in the ignition of the moped. Noooooooooo!

It was early morning when I started my trip back to work. I hated the fact that I had not slept and faced another long duty. All the crew were tucked up in the hotel at Heathrow and I was still messing about. I needed the keys as the bunch had the locker key with my uniform for my duty at work. I used our only car; gave Sarah some taxi money and headed for the 'crime scene again.' I say this; as at night it did feel odd, creeping in the dark undergrowth by the motorway looking for my keys. It also felt wrong running across the motorway. I actually ran across the M25 to save time as the moped was on the other side of the carriageway going back. Now this is not easy as there was a barrier to climb over in the middle.

I did half expect to be seen on one of those reality series that show silly people, running around on motorways.

I never did recover the C90 as it would be dangerous to retrieve the moped from the motorway. How embarrassing would it be; to go to a bungalow in Byfleet knock on the door and ask "Can I have my moped back?" How would we get it back over the nine foot fence anyway?

Today, I hope it rests in peace and acts as a trellis for natural fauna and is a home to a family of wrens.

At the same time we took on a 'rescue dog' Toffee. He was a silver fawn whippet.

The Accident still blew grey clouds into our lives and I felt we needed a focus. We lived with lovely walks all around us and so we decided to allow a 'wolf' into our house! I say this because neither of us had had a dog before and we were a little scared of it all. Toffee; our chosen 'wolf specie' was quite the opposite too our worries. He was relaxed and calm and showed us just how easy dog ownership could be. He went with us pretty much everywhere. Having said this he was the exception as opposed to the rule in behaviour. I mean, it was years before we heard him bark and this came as quite a shock!

The only odd thing to overcome from his past was that he had been raced in some professional way. He had not been walked on a lead and when we *did* let him off the lead, he took off at 35mph in a straight line! Walking him could be very lonely and he ended up about two miles away without the energy to stand up. So with this in mind I found an enclosed field that I could use, with the farmers permission. This field was huge with access to the road on the far end. Toffee ran and ran, so I took to fetching him using the wheel barrow as he was too heavy to carry back home.

The neighbours knew we had a new dog and were not experienced in this area of life. So what the neighbours saw was; me walking up the road with Toffee in the wheel barrow. They could not see him run and then collapse with exhaustion. Several village folk leaned out of their car windows on the road back to say "You're supposed to walk it on a lead!" and other such quips. He was very well behaved and enjoyed the barrow ride home.

Toffee took a few months to work out he could run any time and with the aid of a treat would return with enough energy to walk home. He was a good, loyal friend and helped us in a bad emotional time to recover some, with the help of nature's path.

We moved from Sussex to Cornwall on a whim.

One spring day we were exchanging and completing house deeds on a mobile phone, swopped for a bicycle, driving to Cornwall! Sounds strange but we decided to move to Cornwall as we heard it was a nice place to visit. The reason to move house was; mainly for the fun of exploring somewhere completely new and partly to start again with life. There was no urgency about it only things happened fast, as our house in Burpham Arundel attracted a quick sale. We chose a fishing village, as it could not be compared to the rural country views we already had. You see, we could see Arundel castle from our house and had a 'picture postcard view' at every turn. Now, we would have a *coastal* postcard view at every turn, in Polperro.

It was an exciting place to live and the idea of moving paid off in many ways. We both fell in love with Cornwall as a county as it has more nature in control than some counties 'up country' say. Life is harder for secular work and the distance of the county does show in these matters, but in balance it suited us both more. We soon felt settled and happy enough to think about having a baby. Our new son Harry was born Cornish and spent his early life in Polperro. Life here had some small adventures and tales. I don't want to be blown too far from flying, only to say that next door had a 200 ton land slide! This rock and soil had to be dug out by hand, taking six months or so. We had stories doing up the house and of Sarah working in the village. It was great to see the sea every day and learn the new ways of a tiny fishing port with shop keepers and restaurateurs alike.

To round up the time in B.A. it was ups and downs excuse the pun.

Life away from family has a penalty with ones heart being low. It is the sort of job a single person fairs better on. The stress increased with terrorism after the 9/11 twin tower attacks. We had sympathiser groups days later; stick 'box cutting blades' to a toilet ceiling with masking tape on my flight and we found a handle to complete the knife in another toilet. Bearing in mind the crew in the 9/11 attacks had their throats cut it was stressful for the crew.

The flight deck doors were locked in flight, cutting off the flight crew in a social way slightly and things were never quite the same. We had more and more IFE entertainment systems added to aircraft that were not designed for it. Electrical fires; all be it small, were now a constant worry. This with the usual tech problems like engine failure etc. all helped keep the stress to a *medium* level let's say.

Having said all this, B.A. is one of the best run airlines for safety and most other things, Period. I learnt a lot about the industry and its difficulties.

We had highs as well as lows in the business. I managed to save two lives on board the aircraft. One being a heart attack with CPR being used to good effect and the other was a diabetic coma that went really bad. Helping to get the guy back was 'full on,' but it was rewarding to be able to make a difference when it mattered. In a bizarre twist I also managed to restrain a schizophrenic with hand cuffs who was setting fire to a 777 toilet, with a safe outcome for all on board. You don't do that sort of thing with a desk job, so it was all life experience. As B.A. crew, we saw countries cultures and life, in all its complex way. It was part of travel and part of being crew on the long haul aircraft. It was a pleasure 'to fly to serve' and to see the world.

Sarah and I did later enjoy several trips adding to the stories. With B.A. we went to India, Rome, Cairo and an island in Malaysia.

To finish off motorcycling, I rode about two hundred thousand miles in all weathers with only one slight wobble at 10mph.

Mind you it was not all skill I think some of it was luck too. You are so vulnerable on a bike. They are good for beating traffic and crunching miles though. I think motorcycle choice and riding tuition are important to safe travel, as is top quality clothing. I used electric gloves to keep my 'stopping fingers' ready for action at all times. I rode with the 'stickiest tyres' on light weight excellent handling bikes. I hung off the bike and moved my body around for balance turning the whole thing into a hobby. I ride no more as I think by never getting on a bike again I'm a winner. I have gambled and won in the stakes of motorcycling at least.

With the move to Cornwall's fishing village Polperro, my motorcycles would now carry me all the way from Cornwall, to work at Heathrow it is here the mileage really racked up.

One night the A303 was shut due road works. As it was about four in the morning I went to the road sign and rode beyond to the work. You see, 'the divert' was eight miles and I might just squeeze through the work being on a bike. I did just that which saved lots of valuable time. Next trip things had moved on, I did the same thing this time emergency stopping as the road ran right out. A land slide had made the road unstable and it had been removed with a 15ft drop. I only just stopped in time, it was well, very humbling. I always obey the divert signs now even on a bike!

My motorcycle 'spill story' is a tiny one. I used to call into Popham airfield for coffee on the way up. This was a welcome break and a comfort as it had a good atmospheric club room. On the parameter road diesel was spilt and I missed it. I fell over at about 10mph bending up the brake pedal and smashing in a spark plug. I was aware of the cash penalty of being late and used a rock to smash the brake pedal semi straight. I continued to Heathrow with one cylinder working on the Moto Guzzi it held up well. Fuel on my boot and the return journey to look forward to, was some of the difficulties endured trying to cover the huge miles.

On one ride home, I was so tired I was nodding off on the bike. This is very hard to do on a noisy bike travelling at speed. Usually adrenaline kicks in and with a little help from the 'Red Bull' drink, all things are possible. But, this day I was *mega* tired. I pulled over into a lay-by to dose. Not easy, but remember I was very, very tired. I used my helmet as a pillow and lay near my bike so that it could not be stolen without me knowing about it. I was soon awoken by a boot in my side. I looked up to see a fellow oily biker smoking a roll up saying; "You all right mate?" "Yes I was just trying to dose" I said, much to his puzzlement. He thought I'd hurt myself and had collapsed by the bike.

I found a much more suitable field and dozed right off. When I woke up my bike had fallen over and the visor had given me some sun burn to my face. I had left my helmet on and the visor shut, being so tired. I was refreshed enough by the small sleep to carry on but now had to find oil for the bike, as some had leaked out when it fell over.

That was about all my bike stories, only to say it was also fun getting to Heathrow finding a toilet and changing into a smart steward. Not everyone knew my other side! Now back to flying and 'life after B.A.'

To round up life, I remain happily married and deeply in love.

Sarah is going to University and I'm in a support role to her, as she was for me in the B.A. days. We have one happy healthy son called Harry. We care for another rescue whippet oddly called Mouse. We still live in Cornwall and love the peace and quiet of this county.

My parents live back where it all started in Lincolnshire and enjoy a rural peace. My Brother Grant lives in Horley near the airport with a keen interest in building. Sarah's family are still living where the children grew up in Worthing by the sea.

Sadly, my twin brother died and shall always be missed. He did live his life with lots stories of his own to tell, but some difficulties later overpowered him.

Life is full of strange ups and downs twist and turns, it becomes hard to fathom the more the journey unfolds. Looking back over it all; perhaps we are not meant to fathom it out, perhaps we are meant to live, and enjoy our lives best we can.

I remain thankful, aware of the chance of it all and humbled by what I don't know.

And on flying?

Tiger Moth

I did fly a Tiger Moth in WW2 training livery; with Martin a while back and he wrung it out, as only Martin could. This so far has been my last full size flight, which was a gift from my old friend. I'm getting a little older myself now and a little fussy. If ever I *did* fly full size again, it would have to be a well maintained vintage aeroplane. Preferably open cockpit. The 'Tiggy' flight could well be the very last full size flight, as the family now requires more of my support and the need to fly is less now. But; flying free up high, because you want to and going where one pleases will always be a special memory. To help describe this I have adapted this poem to try to capture the experience.

The last sentence evokes a feeling of presence for which we are mere mortals. I did see how high I could go in the VP1 and rose right next to a billowing white Cumulus Nimbus cloud. You know; those 'monster clouds' that are quite dangerous to be around when active. This thing was enormous, some 18,000ft tall and it was blinding white always towering above me. I could see my aeroplanes shadow, chasing around, on the shape of this monster cloud in full sun. As I rose I did feel I was in completely another world and one I was not invited into. It made me think of a powerful creator and his mighty world. The experience sent a chill into me that day and made me slightly question if it is right that we should fly?

'Who is to say?' only this amazing experience will always be remembered.

> Oh! To slip the surly bonds of earth
> and dance with clouds of laughter and tumbling mirth.
>
> Upwards to climb and do a hundred things you have not dreamed of. To wheel, turn and spin high in the sunlit silence. Hovering there, where neither lark or eagle dare.
>
> I've chased the shouting wind along, and flung my eager craft through footless halls of air.
>
> Up up the long delirious burning blue, in sanctity and space I've topped the wind-swept heights with easy grace.
>
> And yet, all the while with silent lifting mind I've trod reached out my hand and touched the face of God.

None of this reflective emotion is in loss; I hasten to add, because I still get a 'fix' with radio control model aircraft even to this day.

You see with models you can have the flight interest with easy building experimentation as well. The consequences of error are not so harsh, so in fact, stress levels are lower than in full size aviation. The funds needed to do it, fit better in a family budget.

We enjoy flying large model gliders off the cliff using the lift generated by the sea wind. Living in Cornwall, the free flying sites are all around. Throw in fresh air, good scenery, great friends and it is quite a heady mix of fun. Life can be hard at times and it is good to take time to relax. I can enjoy a good days model flying and always come back feeling better. We have a 'squadron' of like minded chaps and wander round Cornwall like something from the sitcom 'last of the summer wine.'

I encourage beginners to fly in any way they can and always try to offer help. The gift of flight is a wonderful thing and something marvellous to share. Our beginner's models sometimes land up in bushes or trees and we return to our youth in getting them down. The days are always fun and sentiments of such, echo in this poem to conclude.

Across the fields of yesterday,

He sometimes comes to me,

The boy just back from play,

The boy I used to be.

Wishing you highs, to overcome life's lows,

Lloyd.